If Only I Could

Read Music

C. Harry Causey

For further information, you may contact the publisher as follows:

Music Revelation
7 Elmwood Court
Rockville, Maryland 20850-2935
(301) 424-2956

Table of Contents

Introduction

It was the worst moment of the day — maybe of the entire week. The acknowledged leaders of the softball teams stood like two Presidential candidates waiting for the debates to begin. Then, as the rest of us stood expectantly, waiting to hear how the matter would be resolved, team members were chosen one by one.

The best were always the first to get the nod. Then came the better batters, the better runners. Finally, both sides resolved to just make the best of it, and the rest of us were chosen.

Looking down at the dusty playing field beneath our feet, we tried not show how much it hurt. This was the weekly ritual of humiliation, courtesy of our elementary school physical education requirements. This was the moment when that extraordinary gong inside my heart pounded with undeniable guilt — I was a wimp. I couldn't bat. I couldn't run. I should have been the water boy.

You know you can't play softball when you're not chosen for the team. You know you can't fly when you jump off your roof. So what does this have to do with the choir? Well, you know you can't read music when the director shouts "piano," and you glance over at the keyboard. You know you can't read music when your neighbor turns your anthem right side up for you. You know you can't read music when you're on page seven singing "Coda" while everyone else is back on page two.

You want to sing. You want to sing well. But here you go again — back to that weekly ritual of humiliation, courtesy of your church choir rehearsal. You don't know "g sharp" from "adagio." You don't know a half note from a half truth. But God has placed the song in your heart, so you try not to appear lost.

You sit tolerantly as the director explains what he or she wants you to do with those dots and lines and funny squiggles before your eyes. You have a plan: You'll just do whatever the rest of your section does — hoping they have some clue as to what's next.

Reading music is not that difficult. Learning the basics will give you enormous freedom in your rehearsals and worship services. You won't have to fear not being chosen for the team anymore. You'll be able to hold your head high when you go to the locker room — make that the robing room — with the rest of your team.

Music is loosely defined as "organized sound." "Sound" you know about: "Organized" is the problem. All you have to do is this — get a grasp of how the plan works and learn a little vocabulary. That's what this book is all about — the plan and the vocabulary. You just have to use it.

That's where your part is essential — you must apply what you learn here. Little by little, you should start finding your pitch. You should start singing melodies without the piano pounding it out for you. You should know what line or page the rest of the choir is on. You should start having more music fun.

And music is fun. You already enjoy it, or you wouldn't put yourself through the rigors of rehearsals every week. You can't imagine how much more fun it's going to be when you really know what you're doing.

There are three primary elements of music — melody, rhythm, and harmony. For the average church choir member, there's the need to learn about only the first two — melody and rhythm. We'll leave harmony for the director and accompanists. Let's keep it as simple as possible and get you on the path to reading music with ease.

Four-Part Harmony

That harmony of which we spoke is achieved when all the voice parts in the choir work together. There are four of them — soprano, alto, tenor, and bass. That's assuming, of course, that your church has a group of both men and women willing to commit to the ministry of music in the choir. And that's assuming further that at least a few of those guys are tenors. At any rate, if you are a complete complement of voices, those are the four categories. You fit into at least one of them comfortably.

Soprano and alto are the respective high and low parts for the ladies; tenor and bass are the respective high and low parts for the guys. Which of those four voice parts is yours? Perhaps you think you are a soprano, but you really ought to be singing alto. The problem is you can't read the alto part, so you continue to struggle with notes too high for you. That's common. Or perhaps you just don't know where your voice correctly lies. Your choir director should be able to guide you in that decision; but by the time you finish this book, perhaps you'll be able to do it for yourself.

The good news is that it's not absolutely necessary for a bass to be able to navigate the soprano part. It's not absolutely necessary for an alto to be able to read tenor, either. There are different problems for each of those vocal sections of the choir. This book will isolate information for the various voice parts so you can learn just what you have to know. Of course, you can be industrious and learn about your neighbor's musical territory as well. You decide.

Those four voice parts — soprano, alto, tenor, bass — are often abbreviated "SATB." So whenever you see SA in this book, think female; when you see TB, think male.

Our Plan

We're going to start at the beginning. We're assuming that in spite of your time at bat, you can't hit the ball at all. Even if you know a little about reading music already, you might find the beginning a good place for you to start anyway. We suspect you'll learn a few new things there that will help you follow our map more easily.

We've included lots of musical examples. Almost all of them are from well known hymns or worship songs. When you see printed music in this book, it will probably be a tune you already know in your head. That should make it easier for you to grasp the basic concepts you will need to read unfamiliar music. When you get to the end of our journey, we'll give you some challenges which you should be able to maneuver with a fair amount of confidence.

So now it's just you and this book. Don't sit and read it through. Take it step by step. Go over all the illustrations, even if you think you don't need to. Think about it as you go. Take all the time you need to be comfortable with the material.

When you go to the next rehearsal or worship service, look through the hymnal and anthems. Spot what you've been learning about here. Then smile: You're gonna get chosen for the team!

Chapter 1

Get It in Writing

In the beginning, there were sounds. God's creatures spoke. They communicated. Languages developed, and verbal expression gave way to primitive written systems. From cave walls to the printing press, thoughts were able to be shared in meaningful ways.

In the beginning, there were songs. God's creatures sang. They communicated through music as well as the spoken word. The same needs existed for written communication in this beautiful new language as for those grunts and sputters that were being spoken. From hand signals to engraved print, musical notation evolved. God's people set themselves to the task of getting it in writing. Now we have to read it.

You wouldn't believe how difficult it was to read the first musical notations. Thank God we have developed a system that is more practical than those first efforts. Let me explain.

Men realized that the musical sounds they were making — both vocally and through their primitive musical instruments — had varying highs and lows. They didn't understand the concept of "pitches" yet, but they were creating them all day long anyway.

As their vocal cords vibrated more rapidly, the resulting sounds were higher in pitch. When they pounded the largest hollow tree trunks, the resulting sounds were lower in pitch. Visually, men could imagine going up for the sounds with faster vibrations and turning down again for the slower ones.

In an effort to capture this in writing, the concept of a ladder was invented. The slow vibrations of the low tones were on the bottom of the ladder; the rapid vibrations of the high tones received top placement. Using little square markings, it might have looked like this:

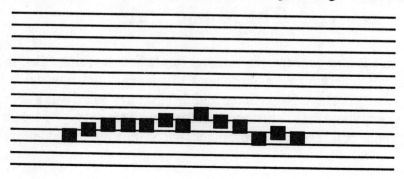

It seemed like a good idea to give the rungs of the ladder names. Not to waste parchment, the spaces between the rungs also received names. Translated into our modern alphabet, the result looked like this:

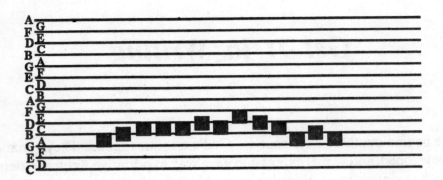

You may have noticed that the names of those rungs (lines) and spaces went from "A" to "G." Then they start repeating themselves. Don't worry about why. Just know that you are only going to have to learn eight letters of the alphabet. See how easy this is going to be?

Now imagine how much more complex primitive musical notation became when the song was long. And what if they wanted to sing in harmony, combining their lovely highs and rich lows. Notated on their musical ladder, the result would have been truly remarkable.

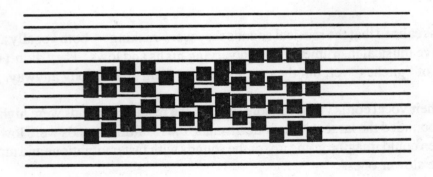

Confusing? You bet. Somebody had to invent a better mouse trap for this early choir. So somebody did, and the musical staff we know and love today was finally born.

The Music Staff

Taking this ladder concept, our musical forefathers just simplified the whole mess. The keyboard was emerging as a prominent instrument, and musical notation for the keyboard was greatly desired. Right in the middle of the keyboard was a note with the name of "C." Don't worry about that — just accept it for now. This note — "Middle C" — seemed like a good reference point not only on the piano, but on the musical ladder itself. To indicate its location, they came up with a great idea. They eliminated the ladder's rung at "Middle C," but imagined the line to still be there, and placed it on the box that represented that pitch instead. It looked like this:

Then somebody noticed that it was hard (or actually impossible) to sing all the notes on the ladder. So early musicians started doing the same thing with the other ladder rungs at the bottom and top. The resulting notation as even easier to read:

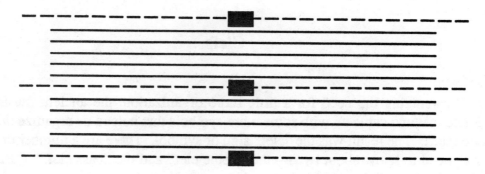

Add a line on the left side to help group things together a bit, and you have what we all recognize as our modern musical staff:

The staff is now is defined as having five lines (no longer rungs) and the four spaces between them. The "Grand Staff" is the joining of two staves -- basically one for the guys and one for the ladies — with that line on the left connecting them. "Middle C" is right in the middle. Convenient? To make it prettier and also give it some more needed organization, a brace or bracket was added. Now we have this:

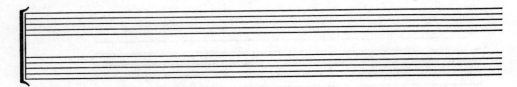

The imaginary lines — the ones that aren't there but really are — are called "leger lines." That's also spelled "ledger" in older traditions. The pronunciation is clearer in the older spelling: The vowel of the first syllable is as in the word "led."

So on our music staff, we have lots of imaginary lines — leger lines. Maybe you didn't know they were there, but they are. That famous "Middle C" is represented by one of them, and all those pitches that fall above or below the staff are covered by the rest. Later on, we'll learn about some of those notes that fall above or below the staff since singers have to recognize two or three of them. But for now, we'll learn a few more important symbols.

Clefs

Recognizing the need for a little more organization, the ancient music notation committee met and came up with some more symbols that helped us organize this musical ladder or staff. The result was the "clef" sign or symbol. There are a number of them, but you only need to know about two — the "treble clef" and the "bass clef." ("Bass" is not pronounced like the fish, but like the word "base.") You've seen these thousands of times. They look like this:

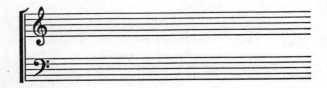

The treble clef is primarily for the women's voices — soprano and alto. So you ladies really have to learn only the treble staff. The bass clef is for the lowest part in the choir — the bass section. That reference to "lowest" has to do with pitch, guys. Don't get insulted or anything. You basses only have to learn the bass clef. Anything we can do to make this easier — right?

You'll notice the tenors were not mentioned. That's because the poor tenors have the unique privilege of having to learn both the treble and bass clefs. You have to have a higher IQ (not to mention a higher voice) to be a tenor. Hold your heads high and your chests out, guys.

Why do the tenors have this singular privilege? Well, you'll find in all hymnals and in much of the printed choral music that the tenor part is written just above the bass part in the bass clef. However, in many octavos (that's an in-house word for printed anthem), when the four voice parts are separated into four staves, the tenor part is written in the treble clef. Don't ask me why, fellows: It's one of the crosses you have to bear for being so needed (and appreciated) in the choir.

When we offer you musical examples in this book, we'll usually give them to you in both the treble and bass clefs. Just pick the one or ones you want to practice and learn. If you can, learn both; but specialize in the one that affects you the most. Tenors, go for broke — learn both.

Every Good Boy ...

What are the names of all those lines and spaces in the modern staff? They're labeled for you below, but you will find it very helpful to learn what most first-year piano students are taught — acronyms for each of the lines and spaces for each clef. First, the labels.

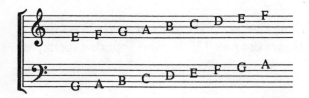

Always read from the bottom of the staff. The treble staff lines are ...

F

D

B

G

E

The most popular acronym for these lines is **"Every good boy does fine."** We could make up a new one, get even cuter, or even get spiritual about it. But perhaps we're all better off learning what everybody else who speaks this language already knows — "Every good boy does fine."

Say it aloud few times. Point to the lines on the treble staff, always starting from the bottom. Then point to them and substitute the letter names of the lines — **"E G B D F."** You should chant this little formula almost religiously until you know it as well as your home telephone number. Then move on to the spaces.

The spaces in the treble staff are the easiest to remember — **F A C E**. Would that all the lines and spaces spelled English words this easily.

Now let's move to the bass staff. The lines are ...

A
F
D
B
G

The most popular acronym for these is "**Good boys do fine always.**" Try it. Chant "**G B D F A**" as above. Practice saying that when you're shaving or driving or showering or whenever you think about it.

Then add the spaces of the bass clef ...

G
E
C
A

There are two popular acronymns here. The first is, "**All cows eat grass.**" As times changed, a second popular one developed—"**All cars eat gas.**" Either one sounds expensive to me, so take your pick, guys.

Once you get your good boys, your faces, and your cows (or cars) firmly planted in your mind, you are ready to progress to a true test. You know you can read music when you are able to skip around at random through those five lines and four spaces, calling out the correct name without really thinking about it. That takes practice. If you skip this step (who's looking - Right?), you'll be sorry later. It's like trying to learn to write sentences before you've mastered the alphabet.

We've included some practice pages for you here. There's a blank staff—no labels to help you cheat—with which you may practice until your heart's content. Do it now, but come back to it tomorrow and the day after and the day after and .... Just take your finger or perhaps a pencil and randomly point to a line or space. Call out the letter. Then, if you need to, test your accuracy by using your appropriate acronym.

After that, we have some fun exercises using notes on the staff that spell words. Yes, we know — you had to do that in school during the days when you still had recess. It was invented as a child's game to help learn those lines and spaces, so we've included a few adult words to keep you interested. Don't worry: This is a Christian book. We've even included some spiritual thoughts. Have fun.

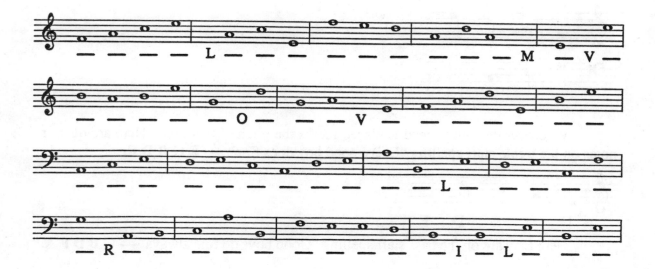

How did you do? Here are the answers:

Treble Clef: *Face, lace, fed, Adam, Eve, babe, God, gave, fade, be*
Bass Clef: *Ace, decade, able, deaf, grab, cab, feed, Bible, be*

Musical Notes

Getting it in writing was a long process for those early musicologists. Some of the symbols they created were clever, but they were not all that easy to read. Square shapes meant one thing and diamond shaped ones meant another. A line here or there or a cluster of black markings indicated that the voice was supposed to perform certain notes around the symbols. Today's music students spend months learning all about it just so they can appreciate the relatively simple notation that's evolved for you and me.

Right now, we are going to learn about only one note — one symbol. It's the most common of them all, and it's called the "quarter note." It looks like this:

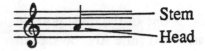
— Stem
—Head

This symbol has two primary parts — the note **head** and the **stem**, as labeled above. It can appear on your staff with the stem facing up or down, depending on where it falls on the staff. Notice that it is black (filled in) on the note head. Some other notes are not, as we will see later.

Wherever the note's head is placed marks the pitch of that note. Here are quarter notes on the treble staff spelling "Every good boy does fine" — **E G B D F.**

Here they are on the bass staff spelling "Good boys do fine always" — **G B D F A.**

That's all we're going to learn about notes for now. With the quarter note as your friend, let's move on to something you can sing.

Scales

Just as our alphabet is the starting place for verbal communication, musical scales (no, they have nothing to do with fish) are the starting place for musical performance. These are our building blocks.

There's enough information about scales to fill a month or two of classes, but you don't need all that to navigate through the music. What you do need, however, is a good working knowledge of the most common scale in music — the "major scale."

Before we introduce that, let's give you a simplified definition. A musical scale is an arrangement of eight consecutive pitches either in ascending or descending order.

The song "Do Re Mi" from THE SOUND OF MUSIC is one of the most notable examples of a musical scale to be found. Thanks to Mary Martin and Julie Andrews, even the musically deprived can sing, "Do, Re, Mi, Fa, Sol, La, Ti, Do."

Here is a familiar example of a scale found in Christian literature. You've sung it for years, but you may not have realized you were actually singing a descending major scale. Don't worry about the other musical notation you see here: Just sing the melody and hear the scale.

There are some notes that don't fall on the staff lines or spaces, so we labeled them for you. Take note of them, because they will be showing up again soon.

Now sing it on "la, la, la" and listen to these eight pitches. Then try to sing it backwards — "Come is Lord the world the to Joy." Stick to "la, la" — it's much easier! That is the ascending scale.

Notice it starts on "C" and ends on "C." As in the song, "Do Re Mi," the first and last notes of the scale have the same name. Yes, one is higher than the other, but they still have the same name. These beginning and ending notes of the scale identify the scale's name. This example is the C Major Scale. If we had begun and ended on "D," we would be singing the D Major Scale, etc. We'll get into that in more depth later.

Now we're going to do something that is very important for you to grasp. We're going to paint by numbers, if you will. Each note of the scale has a number from 1 to 8. In "Joy to the World," the numbers are in reverse order — 8 down to 1. Here is the same scale in ascending order:

Sing this ascending C Major scale using numbers. Forget "la, la;" and forget words. Use the numbers as they correspond to the notes and listen to yourself sing as you go up the ladder.

Did you do it? If not, go back. You're going to need this skill in pages to come.

A major scale is not just eight consecutive notes as we told you earlier. We said that was a simplified definition. You see, there is a certain pattern to those eight notes that you should know about.

All scales are composed of notes that move in what we call "steps." Wonder if that has anything to do with the old ladder form of notation? Well, as we are climbing Jacob's has anything to do with the old ladder form of notation? Well, as we are climbing Jacob's ladder (couldn't resist), here are the arrangements of steps you need to know about. There are "whole steps" and "half steps." As the names imply, it takes two half steps to make a whole step. Logical.

Using the numbers to identify the eight tones, there are two places where you find half steps in a major scale. Those are between steps 3-4 and between 7-8.

You need to hear the difference between these two important building blocks — the whole step and the half step. To help, let's introduce another Christmas carol that uses a descending scale, but with a different twist. Again, ignore the other musical notation you see for now. Here it is.

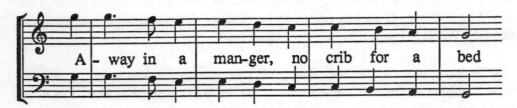

In this example, we again have a C major scale. But notice that it doesn't begin and end on "C" which would correspond to 8 down to 1. In this example, we begin on 5, go through 1, and end on 5. It's still the C major scale, however — just rearranged slightly. Sing this familiar carol on "la, la," and notice the stepwise progression of the notes outlining a major scale.

The numbers are a little different here, too. Since there are only eight notes in a scale, when we count backwards from 5 to 1, we have to start over. But 1 is the same as 8 (the pitch "C"), so we have to go from 1 to 7 as we progress down the staff. You'll get used to it.

Now, here is your assignment. Slowly, carefully sing the first two notes of "Joy to the World." Use "la, la." Listen to yourself. Now sing the first two notes of "Away in a Manger." Again use "la, la." Hear the difference? The first one ("Joy to the World") goes from 8 to 7, or a half step; the second one ("Away in a Manger") goes from 5-4, or a whole step. There is a subtle, yet big difference in the sounds of those two steps.

To help you really feel the difference, try this. After listening to the whole step that begins "Away in a Manger," try singing "Joy to the World" again — but start with a whole step. Sounds strange, doesn't it? Do it several times. Listen. Cringe. Listen. Cringe. Now

Singing by the numbers is going to be our primary method of learning to read music. You only have to learn the eight notes of the scale to do that. Yes, there are subtleties and deviations that will throw curves along the way; but most of the music you have to sing in the average church music program is based on this one friendly pattern — the major scale.

Things to Remember

SATB
Staff
Middle C
Leger (Ledger) lines
Treble clef
Bass clef
"Every Good Boy Does Fine"
"FACE"
"Good Boys Do Fine Always"
"All Cows Eat Grass" - "All Cars Eat Gas"
Quarter note
Major scale
Whole step
Half step

Chapter 2

Name That Tune

Place all the tones of a scale into a jar and shake vigorously. Now pour them out on the printed page. What do you have? Probably a tune that sounds like it was composed by a committee. Deliver us.

Now take all the tones of a scale, put them in the hands of a skilled composer, and pour them out on the printed page. What do you have? A melody — one of the three primary elements of music.

A melody is a pleasing, orderly arrangement of notes in a sequence. The result is a song — something you can whistle in the shower. It's the tune — the lead part.

Yes, it's the sopranos who usually get to sing the melody. Being the easiest part to learn, the sopranos have less need to read music than the rest of the choir — or so they think. They can't help the fact that they get to sing the melody most of their lives, leading to numbness of the musical ear. Give the melody to the altos or the guys for a few lines, throw in something that's non-melody for the sopranos, and watch them squirm.

If you're not a soprano, you are still singing melodies. No, your part does not sound like the lead. It's not the tune. Shower whistling of the alto line is a rare occurrence. Nevertheless, your part is a pleasing (hopefully), orderly arrangement of notes in a sequence. If all is going well, those notes do make sense. At least they make sense to somebody, and our goal is to have them make sense to you. The rules that apply to understanding and reading the melody in the soprano part are the same rules all the other singers in the choir need to successfully execute their vocal part. You just have to learn to read melodies that are not necessarily the main tune or lead part.

For now, we're going to stick to melodies that are the main tune. Your goal is to learn the principles that make those melodies function so that you can later apply that knowledge to whatever is put before you.

Let's go back to "Joy to the World." As we know, it starts with a descending scale — consecutive notes arranged with whole steps and half steps in just the right places. But what happens next? It skips upward by five notes. Then it completes the scale in ascending motion. Look at it. Remember: We're ignoring any other musical notation you see there. Just study the melody.

Now let's add numbers to that.

Sing this melody aloud, using those numbers. If you did not know this melody so well, you might choke when you arrived at that skip on the word "let." What would you do in that case? Well, pretend that you don't know this melody. You're singing it for the first time using numbers. You start with 8 and work your way down the scale to 1. You're at our friendly middle C on the word "come." As quickly as possible, calculate the number of the next pitch (the "G" on "let"). Yes, it's OK at this point to use your finger or a pencil and count lines and spaces. Eventually, however, we want you to be able to look and leap.

Since we've already given you the answer, you know the next number is 5. Now quietly or even silently sing the scale from 1 upward until you reach 5. One of the best methods for doing this is to whistle the melody very quietly. That way you can physically hear it. Leave the lips relaxed so this whistle is almost inaudible to anyone else but you. Try it.

When you reach the fifth degree and know where that pitch is, sing 5 aloud and continue up the scale — 5-6, 6-7, 7-8. Not only do we have an ascending scale here, but now we have an example of one of composers' greatest gifts to struggling music readers — repetition. We saw it in "Away in a Manger," too, but we weren't ready to mention it then. Look at those repeated notes. They're marked for you below:

Whenever you have repeated notes, repeat them. Does that sound stupid, or what? It's true, however, that many folks don't think about what they're doing when trying to read music. As a result, they miss the easiest parts. Concentrate.

One of the prime advantages of repeated notes is that you can sing them almost mindlessly (dangerous word) while your eyes move on to the next note. That's called reading ahead. The more you do it, the better reader you will become. Look ahead. Always look ahead. Right now, rejoice when you are able to see just one note ahead. Eventually, when you get some real practice with this, you can look three or four notes ahead with no problem.

Before we go on, let's mention something else about that skip in "Joy to the World." We jumped from 1 up to 5. Right? There's a name for that skip. It's called a 5th. Makes sense. As we go along, we are going to introduce you to most of the skips you're going to encounter and some quick ways to program your brain for response.

Let's move on to some other melodies that you probably already know. Let's see what makes them tick. We've included the scale degree numbers for the one below. We used only quarter notes this time, so it will look different from what you usually see in your hymnal. Try to identify it without cheating.

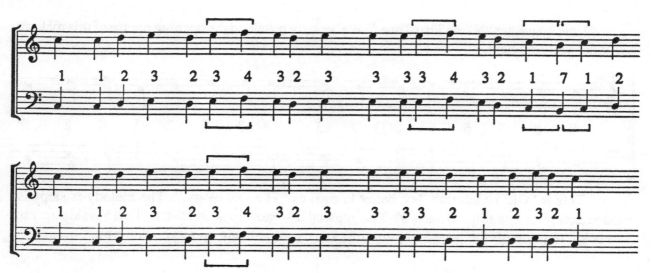

Got it? The name of this tune is "Hamburg." You know it, however, by its more familiar name, "When I Survey the Wondrous Cross."

There are several things we want to point out about this melody. First, it begins on 1 — the first degree of the major scale. Next, it is all stepwise motion — there are no skips in it at all. Next, it uses only five different notes — from 1 up to 4 in the scale and the note just below 1 (which, as we've already noted, is the 7th degree of the scale or number 7). We've marked the half step between 1 and 7. All the rest are whole steps. It's a very tame, unassertive melody; but it really works.

Here's the opening part of another one. It has a skip right after the three repeated notes at the beginning. If you need to, whistle down the scale to find that fourth note. Sing this melody, using the numbers.

8 8 8   5 6 7   8 7 6   5   8 7 6   5 6 4 3 2 1

The fancy name for this one is "Ein' Feste Burg." The familiar name is "A Mighty Fortress Is Our God." There are two important skips in it — the one at the beginning from 8 to 5 and another halfway through from 5 to 8. You'll find that relationship — 8-5, 5-8 — to be very common. Sing those skips three or four times right now until your ear says, "Got it." Also, look at the distance on the page between those notes. Really look. Sing and look at the same time. Now your eyes should also be talking to you.

Did you find the descending scale in "A Mighty Fortress?" It's in the second half of the line, beginning with "A bulwark...." This one, however, has a fun little rise in it, unlike "Joy to the World." It goes from 8 <u>down</u> to 5 step by step, then steps <u>up</u> to 6. What follows is a skip down to 4. While the normal scale goes from 5 down to 4, this one goes 5-6-4. Sing through that point several times. Look and listen as you do. (Sounds a little like your mom teaching you how to cross the street, doesn't it?)

Here's another "Name That Tune." We've only provided the opening phrase of this melody. See what you find here.

8 8 7 6 5   8(1) 2 3   3 3 3 2 1 4 3   2

This is "Old Hundredth," or better known as "The Doxology." The melody is stepwise motion except for one skip. What is it? You guessed it — stop, look and listen. That 5-8 skip upward will begin to jump off the page and bite. Just keep your antenna up so you don't miss it.

One more. This is a worship song, not a hymn. Most everybody knows this tune. See if you can read it, using the number system once again.

This one is "God Is So Good." It has some new skips in it which are three notes apart and therefore called thirds. Sing it again with the numbers, but this time notice the neat pattern of notes you hear (and see). The first four notes are sung again, only on higher pitches. Then they are repeated a second time, only higher still. The last five notes of the song bring us back down to the key note of "C."

That repeated pattern of notes is called a "sequence." Like repeated notes, sequential patterns are common in music. They are your friends. Spotting them will help you read more music more quickly. Here they are again, highlighted so you won't miss them.

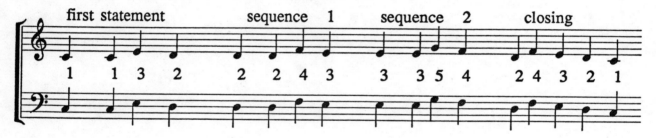

My friend, did you realize you're already reading music? Yes, these melodies present no real challenge yet; but you are indeed beginning to analyze some of the essential elements that make melodies work. In your rehearsals, start looking for scales. Start recognizing that skip from 5 up to 8 or from 8 down to 5. It will get easier as you go and as you learn more.

Things to Remember

Melody
Steps
Skips
8-5, 5-8
Repeated notes
Look ahead
Sequence

Chapter 3

It's About Time

You might remember that we gave you a brief, simplified definition of music as "organized sound." The primary way it is organized is in time. Music is a temporal art. Now for some folks, that's good news. They love numbers, they excelled at arithmetic, and new math was second nature. For others, that's bad news. They can't balance their check book, still use their fingers to add, and the closest they want to come to counting is Sesame Street.

Regardless of your aptitude with numbers, the time factor of music is basically very simple. If you can count to four, chances are pretty good you're going to ripple through this.

The word we're looking for that defines all this is "rhythm" — that second essential element of music. It's the flow of music. It's the heartbeat or pulse. It's the conscious combination of sound durations that make interesting patterns in time.

Now before we go on, here is a challenging observation — one which takes a little bravery to even include. Women seem to have more trouble with rhythm than men. Sorry, ladies, but it's true. The guys seem to like math more in school, too. If you accept this generality, then part of the challenge is for you sopranos and altos to take a little extra care with this subject. And count it all joy! (Pun intended.)

Rhythm in music is organized around "beats." The beat is the pulse of the music. There are strong beats and weak beats, but you don't have to worry too much about those at this point. It's sufficient for you to recognize that beats exist, and we're going to be counting them.

Note Values

The various durations in musical time are expressed by different types of notes. We've already introduced you to the quarter note, mentioning that it is the most common of all. Here are some others that you will encounter along the way. Each of them receives a certain number of beats.

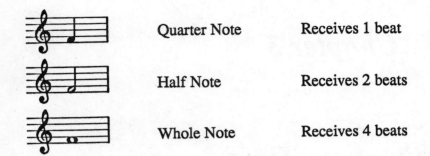

Quarter Note   Receives 1 beat

Half Note   Receives 2 beats

Whole Note   Receives 4 beats

You already understand by their names that the **half note** is one-half the value of the **whole note** (half note = two beats; whole note = 4 beats). It doesn't take much logic to understand, therefore, that the **quarter note** is one-fourth of the whole note (quarter = 1 beat; whole note = 4 beats). It is also one-half of a half note (quarter = 1 beat; half = 2 beats). This is easier to see in diagram form.

Notice that the quarter note and half note each have note heads and stems. Their only difference is that the quarter note's head is filled in while the half note's head is not. The whole note has a note head only — no stem. Some say it looks like a doughnut hole, and they remember its name that way. Sounds fattening; but if it works, we won't knock it.

The Bible, as you know, is divided into little sections called chapters and verses. That makes it easier for us to find our way through it and helps us quickly return to a favorite passage. In a similar way, musical compositions are divided into little sections. But unlike the Bible, where the sections are of varying lengths, music is organized into segments of exactly the same length called "**measures.**" A measure is a prescribed number of **beats**, the most common of which contain 4 beats or 3 beats — in that order.

Measures are notated on the staff by a vertical line called a "**bar line.**" There are always (well, almost always) the same number of beats between each bar line.

Here is an example of measures, each separated by bar lines, each measure containing four beats.

Let's apply this to one of the hymns we explored in the last chapter. In "When I Survey the Wondrous Cross," you'll find four-beat measures containing the three different notes we've discussed so far — quarter, half, and whole.

Counts:

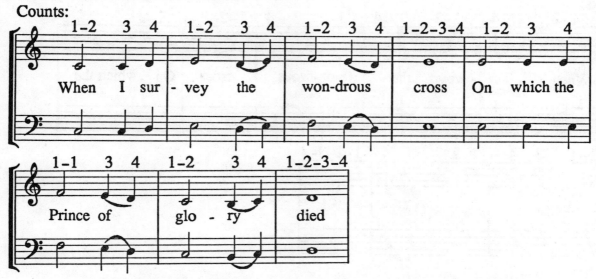

To get the idea of how this thing works, you need to keep a steady beat. In other words, just as the pulse of your body is a steady pulse (hopefully), the pulse of music must be steady. Sometimes it's a fast pulse (running, exercising, praising), and sometimes it's a slow pulse (resting, sleeping, praying). Just keep it steady.

One beat per second is the same as 60 beats per minute. With that guide in mind, count off four or five beats at the speed of one per second. Maybe you've heard the old trick for arriving at that speed by saying aloud and evenly, "One-thousand one, one-thousand two, one-thousand three," etc. This approximates one beat per second.

Now when you sing "When I Survey the Wondrous Cross," keep that steady beat. You can easily sing it at one beat per second. But let's try counting it. Let's see how those beats and measures are put together to make musical sense. The numbers you see below the words are the numbers of the beats in each measure.

When I sur - vey the won - drous cross
1-2 3 4 | 1-2 3-4 | 1-2 3-4 | 1-2-3-4

On which the Prince of glo - ry died
1-2 3 4 | 1-2 3-4 | 1-2 3-4 | 1-2-3-4

Translated back into musical notation, it looks like this:

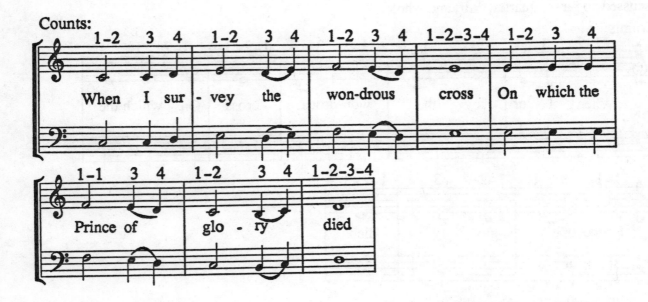

Here is an example of a familiar hymn that uses almost all quarter notes. Sing it through twice. The first time, sing it using scale degree numbers as in the last chapter. The second time, sing it on the counts per measure. When you do, lightly tap your finger on the page under each note to set up the pulse you wish to keep.

O God, Our Help in Ages Past

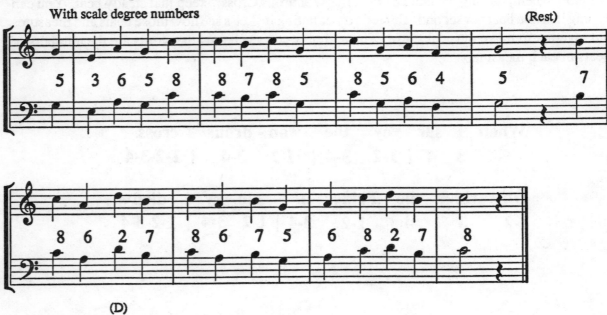

With counts per measure

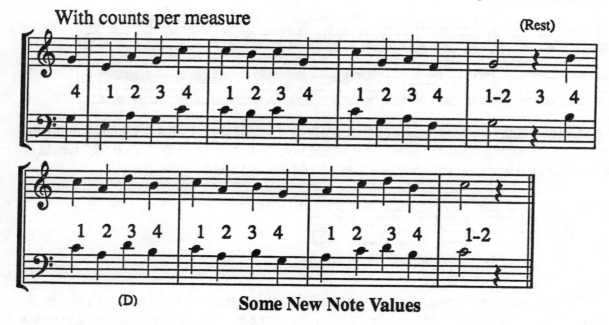

(D)   **Some New Note Values**

There are two other note values that you will need to learn. The first is the **eighth note (8th note)**; the second is the **sixteenth note (16th note)**. They look like this:

The values of these notes are easiest to remember by their relationship to the quarter note. There are two 8th notes in a quarter note; there are four 16th notes in a quarter note.

Why are they called 8th and 16th notes? Because of their relationship to the whole note. It takes eight 8th notes to equal one whole note; it takes sixteen 16th notes to equal the same whole note value. These numbers get larger than the average person can count on their fingers. So we go back to the idea of relating these notes to the quarter note instead of the whole. It's easier.

Perhaps you noticed something new with these notes. Each has an extra extension. In elementary school, the children are taught to call that extension the note's "**flag**." In adultsville, the right word is "**hook**." Call it whatever you prefer: The result is the same. The 8th note has one hook; the 16th note has two.

Since these notes usually come in pairs or quads, it is very common to find them grouped together with another notational device called a "**beam**." This is the process of joining the notes together rather than using all those hooks or flags which confuse the eye. Here's an example of how much better beamed notes appear on the page.

When counting four consecutive quarter notes, you would say, "1 2 3 4." When counting the same measure containing eight 8th notes, you would say, "1 & 2 & 3 & 4 &." That "&" would of course be expressed as the word "and" — "1 and 2 and 3 and 4 and."

When counting 16th notes, the best suggestion we know is to express them as "1 & dee &, 2 & dee &," etc. That gives you something to say for each note, and it flows off the tongue rather easily. It's easier to write as "1 & d &."

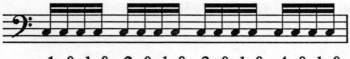

Now lets get sophisticated and mix them up. We've included the counts. If you study them, you'll learn; if you skip over them, you're cheating. (Smile)

Let's turn to a musical example. Check out this melody with scale degree numbers first. Then count it all the way through. We've supplied it three times for you below — once with text only, then with melody scale degree numbers, and finally with the counts. After you've practiced it, go back to the first version without the helps and see if you can do it alone.

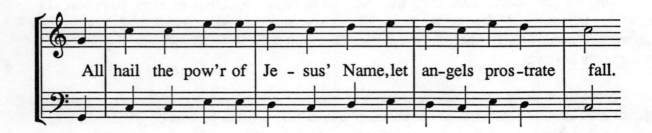

With scale degree numbers

| 5 | 8(1) | 1 | 3 | 3 | 2 | 1 | 2 | 3 | 2 | 1 | 3 | 2 | 1 |

With measure counts

| 4 | 1 | 2 | 3 | 4 | 1 | 2 | 3 | 4 | 1 | 2 | 3 | 4 | 1-2 |

Dots and Rests

Just when you thought it was safe to go on, we have to throw in two more time organizers — "**dots**" and "**rests.**" When learning a new foreign language, there are some vocabulary words you have to learn before you can make good sentences. You are developing a new language — that of music. You are still learning some of those crucial building blocks at this point. If it begins to seem a little overwhelming, take a break and come back to it later. But if you're undaunted, let's move on.

Dots add value to notes. That's often needed to make the rhythm interesting or to make the music fit the rhythm of the words being sung. The amount of time the dot adds to a note is equal to **one-half the value of the note to which it is attached.** So a quarter note increases from one beat to one and one-half beats. A half note increased from two beats to three beats.

The dot is placed to the right of the note's head. Here are some samples.

You'll see better how these work with another musical example. We've been using this one all along, and you already know how to make the dotted rhythms work. Study it a little so you understand it better.

Joy to the World

Now what about rests? **Rests** in music are moments of silence — measured silence. They are not moments when you do nothing: They are instead moments when you perform silence. That's sometimes the best part of music.

There are rests to correspond with each note value. So there are quarter rests, half rests, whole rests, 8th rests, and 16th rests. Here's how they appear.

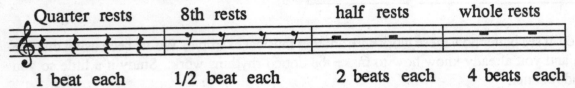

Quarter rests	8th rests	half rests	whole rests
1 beat each	1/2 beat each	2 beats each	4 beats each

Look at this famous example of the use of the quarter rest. The moments of silence here are truly powerful.

Hallelujah from MESSIAH

Hal-le -lu -jah!   Hal-le -lu -jah!   Hal-le -lu -jah!   Hal-le -lu -jah!   Hal-le -lu -jah!

Meter Signature

Finally, we come to that vital piece of information that ties all these rhythmic components together — the **"meter signature."** This is sometimes called the **"time signature."** It appears only at the very beginning of each composition and appears as two numbers, one over the other. There are a variety of these meter signatures, like those that follow:

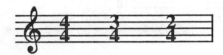

Meter signatures give you two basic details that keep everybody counting the music together. First, you learn **how many beats are to be counted in each measure.** Four beats is the most common, but you can have three or two or six just about as often. The second detail is **what kind of note receives one beat.** The quarter note is by far the most common unit here, but you occasionally see the half note or the 8th note receiving the honors.

Here's how to read the meter signature. The top number equals the beats per measure; the bottom number equals the type of note to receive one beat. The most common meter signature is $\frac{4}{4}$, meaning there are four beats in a measure with the quarter note receiving one beat. Get out your calculator, and you will discover that it takes four quarter notes — each receiving one beat — to complete one full measure in $\frac{4}{4}$ time. Now that's not so hard.

Here are some examples of $\frac{4}{4}$ and $\frac{3}{4}$. Let's get the most out of them we can. Notice everything we've been talking about — meter signature, measures, bar lines, melody, steps, skips, note values, beamed notes, dots, repetition, patterns. We'll help with some pointers along the way.

Meter: 4/4

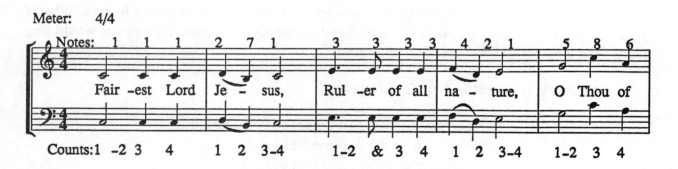

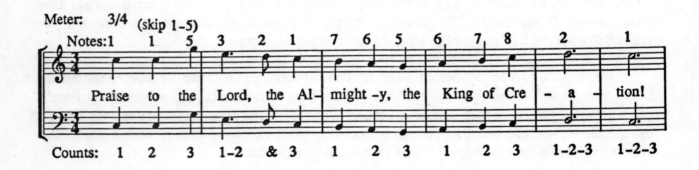

Let's go at this from another angle. Here are the texts to two well known hymns. What is your guess as to the meter signature of each? Read the words in the same rhythm you would sing them. The beats should become obvious to you.

Example 1: Great Is Thy Faithfulness

Chorus: Great is Thy faithfulness! Great is Thy faithfulness!
Morning by morning new mercies I see;
All I have needed Thy hand hath provided -
Great is Thy faithfulness, Lord, unto me.

Example 2: **Holy, Holy, Holy**

> Holy, holy, holy! Lord God Almighty!
> Early in the morning our song shall rise to Thee;
> Holy, holy, holy! merciful and mighty!
> God in three Persons, blessed Trinity.

Example 3: **Faith of Our Fathers**

Verse:
> Faith of our fathers, living still
> In spite of dungeon, fire and sword:
> O how our hearts beat high with joy
> Whene'er we hear that glorious word!

The answers are as follows:

Example 1 is $\frac{3}{4}$ Example 2 is $\frac{4}{4}$ Example 3 is $\frac{3}{4}$

How did you do?

There is just one more meter signature we want to draw to your attention before we leave this subject. You won't encounter it too often, but you will indeed see it at least once a year and probably more often. That's the $\frac{6}{8}$ meter signature.

Now if you remember the formula, that simply means there are six beats in each measure, and the 8th note (not the quarter note for a change) receives one beat. In this scheme, the 8th note has been promoted from its usual place of receiving only half a beat to that of receiving one full beat. Since the 8th note is half the value of a quarter note, the good ole quarter note now gets promoted to two beats instead of one. A typical measure of $\frac{6}{8}$ looks like this:

One of the best examples of this meter is found in just about everybody's favorite Christmas carol, "Silent Night."

Meter 6/8

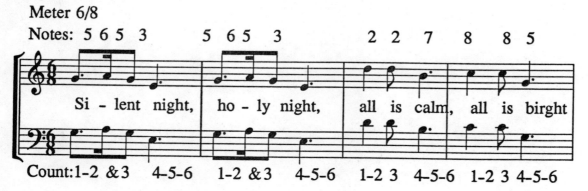

We've included this example just so you'll be equipped to face that day when your choir director throws a $\frac{6}{8}$ meter in your lap and shouts, "Count!" For purposes of your growth in reading music right now, why not look back at "Silent Night" and sing it through using scale degree numbers.

By the way, here's a bonus question: What is the meter signature of "Joy to the World?" The correct answer is $\frac{2}{4}$ — two beats per measure with the quarter note receiving one beat.

If you've made it this far, you should have gained enough tools to make you much more confident as a musician. Granted, there's more; and there will always, always be the need to practice these skills. You can do that now. Take your hymnal, songbook, or anthems home with you. Sit in your favorite chair away from all distractions and start enjoying the freedom of reading music.

Things to Remember

Rhythm
Quarter note
Half note
Whole note
Measure
Bar line
Beat
Steady beat
8th note
16th note
Flag/Hook
Beam
Dots
Rests
Meter signature
$\frac{4}{4}$ $\frac{3}{4}$

Chapter 4

Singing a Different Tune

Remember the C major scale? We've talked about it, analyzed it, and given lots of examples using it. You're going to need to have a firm grip on that scale for what comes next, so let's review.

The **major scale** consists of eight consecutive notes, ascending or descending. There are **whole steps** and **half steps** in the scale. The two half steps fall between the **3rd and 4th** degrees as well as the **7th and 8th** degrees. One more time, here's what it looks like in print.

C Major Scale

Now here's something very important for you to add to your memory banks: The half steps in that C major scale (or any other scale) always fall in the same places on the staff. In the C major scale, they are always between "E" and "F" and between "B" and "C." Look at the staff again and note exactly where those half steps are for your voice part. Memorize it.

Half steps between E-F, B-C

Sharps and Flats

You will recall the C major scale derives its name from the first and last notes of the scale. Now let's look at a new scale. This one is the G scale. As its name implies, it starts and ends on "G."

G scale

G A B C D E F G

Question: Do the half steps (3-4, 7-8) fall in the right places on the staff in this scale? Well, 3-4 is fine ("E" to "F" is a half step), but ouch with 7-8. "F" to "G" — the 7th and 8th degrees of this scale — comprises a whole step. That doesn't fit our formula.

This is where **sharps** and **flats** come in. You've probably heard of them, and you might even recognize them on sight.

Sharp

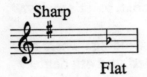

Flat

A sharp raises a pitch by one half step; a flat lowers it by one half step. In order to make the G major scale happy, we need to raise the 7th note one half step so the 3-4, 7-8 rule is satisfied. It looks like this.

G Major Scale

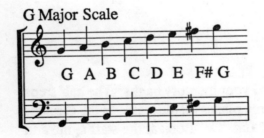

G A B C D E F# G

Key Signatures

Every time we want to write or sing G major, we need an F sharp. Since that's going to take extra effort to write, more ink to print, and create more black marks on the page for our eyes to absorb, a wonderful shorthand method was created. It's called a **key signature.**

In order to indicate the need to raise that "F" by a half step, we place a sharp on the "F" line at the beginning of each line of music — like this:

G Major scale with key signature

G A B C D E F# G

Now we say we are in the key of G major. Here's an example you'll recognize.

The Doxology

We gave you that same example in Chapter 2, but we left it in the key of C major so as not to confuse you. The soprano part looked like this:

In case you didn't already know, that's high enough to rattle the dishes. It lies better in the voice down where it belongs — G major.

So there are different keys. How many are there, you ask? More than you really need to learn. There are, in fact, dozens of them. Here's the good news: To sing most of the literature we use in the church, you really only need to understand seven keys. Notice we didn't say "know" seven keys. That would be the ideal, but you can function pretty well with a basic understanding of the major scale as it begins on seven different notes. That's better than learning dozens of them. Right?

Whenever you wish to write a note that has been altered by a sharp or flat, it's done this way — **F#** (F sharp) or **Bb** (B flat). You'll soon discover that some of the keys even begin on altered notes of this sort and therefore have that sharp or flat symbol as part of their name.

First, we'll give you the list of the seven most frequently used keys in church music. Next, we'll show you what their scales look like. Finally, we'll give you the key signatures for each.

Seven Most Common Keys in Church Music

1. **C major**   No sharps or flats
2. **G major**   1 sharp
3. **D major**   2 sharps
4. **F major**   1 flat
5. **Bb major**   2 flats
6. **Eb major**   3 flats
7. **Ab major**   4 flats

Here are the scales for these seven keys:

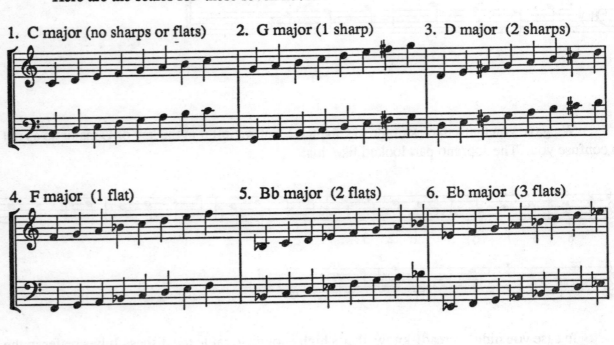

1. C major (no sharps or flats)   2. G major (1 sharp)   3. D major (2 sharps)

4. F major (1 flat)   5. Bb major (2 flats)   6. Eb major (3 flats)

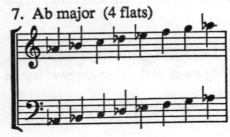

7. Ab major (4 flats)

Now to reduce this to key signatures. It's all the same information, just expressed differently.

This is all understandable. You can grasp it. So what? Here's the kicker: You now need to rethink that scale numbering system you've been learning. In C major, "C" is 1, "D" is 2, etc. In G major, however, "G" is 1, "A" is 2, etc. This is not the way to spell relief!

This will take some practice. In fact, this will take weeks, months, and even years of consistent application before you can really fly through your various pieces of music. It's not unlike learning to speak German or French — you have to use the new language before your confidence level gets beyond total intimidation. No better time to start than right now.

Here is another example from G major -- "Joyful, Joyful, We Adore Thee." We've included the scale degree numbers for a portion of the melody. You fill in the rest.

Joyful, Joyful, We Adore Thee

Key of G major, 4/4 meter signature

[Repeat of first line with slight change at end]

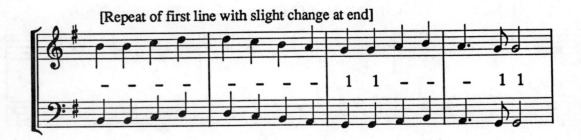

[slight repetition]

[beams]   [beams]

(D)

[repeat of second line]

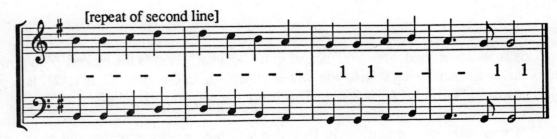

You know what? This works exactly like before when we were in C major. This is still our lovable major scale. The only difference is the starting pitch. We are now in a more singable key for this piece, and you just have to adjust your orientation a little. Think of "G" as 1 (or 8), "A" as 2, "B" as 3, "C" as 4, etc.

Let's try it again. See if you can guess the name of this melody.

Key of G Major, 3/4 meter signature

Did you get it? Amazing! You are well on your way to being the choir director! (For those who are still lost, that was "Amazing Grace.")

Now let's scramble your brain just a little and do the same hymn in another key. This time we will go from one sharp to one flat — the key of F major.

If you are sailing through this without an anxiety attack, you are ready to move ahead. If you are not sure of those last few examples, spend a little more time on them. Reread this section and do the exercises again. Then you'll be ready for the next set of examples.

We are now going to look at music using each of the seven keys. We'll begin with C major, even though we've already given you lots of practice there. It's just nice to have a friend around at times like these. We'll repeat the keys of G major (one sharp) and F major (one flat) just to keep all seven keys in order for you.

Hint: Try writing in the scale degree numbers where you need them. Hum a starting pitch. Any comfortable pitch will do. Then sing through these hymns using the numbers. Whenever there is a sharp or a flat in the music because of the key signature, we've put a sharp or flat symbol above the note off the staff. That's just to point them out to you. You will also find the key notes (1's and 8's) marked to help give you an anchor. Happy sailing.

Christ the Lord Is Risen Today

Key of C Major (no sharps/flats), 4/4 meter signature

(C D E)

O Come, all Ye Faithful

Key of G Major (1 sharp), 4/4 meter signature

Chapter 4: Singing a Different Tune

Jesus Shall Reign

Key of D Major (2 sharps), 4/4 meter signature

My Country, 'Tis of Thee

Key of F Major (1 flat), 3/4 meter signature

The Battle Hymn of the Republic

Key of Bb Major (2 flats), 4/4 meter signature

[Note the extensive use of dotted rhythms.]

Holy, Holy, Holy

Key of Eb Major (3 flats), 4/4 meter signature

(Eb)

To God Be the Glory

Key of Ab Major (4 flats), 3/4 meter signature

Accidentals

Sometimes there is a need for a sharp or flat in the melody, even though it is not found in the key signature. These occurrences are called **accidentals**. Interesting name — they are not accidents at all. They are very deliberate actions by the composer to make the melody move in half steps where needed.

Here are some examples of accidentals in music.

O Little Town of Bethlehem

Key of F major (1 flat), 4/4 meter signature

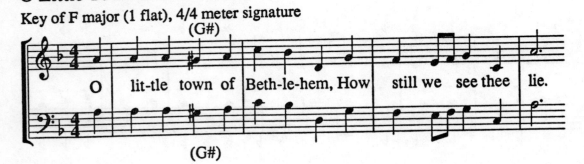

A Mighty Fortress Is Our God

Key of C major (no sharps or flats), 4/4 meter sugnature

O God, Our Help in Ages Past

Key of C major (no sharps or flats), 4/4 meter signature

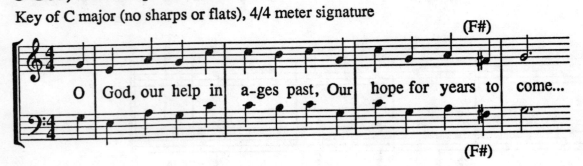

The Natural Sign

One of the special accidentals you will encounter is the **natural** sign. It's there to cancel a sharp or flat in the music. It looks like this:

The Natural Sign

If the note should have been sharped in the first place, the natural lowers it by one half step. If the note should have been flatted, the natural raises it by one half step. So whenever you see a natural in the music, glance over at the key signature. If you are in sharps, the natural is probably lowering a note; if you are in flats, the opposite is true. There's the operative word — opposite. The natural sign has the quality of making the note do the opposite of what it should do according to the key signature.

Here are some examples:

America the Beautiful

Key of Bb major (2 flats), 4/4 meter signature
* Naturals are noted by an asterisk

Crown Him with Many Crowns

Key of D major (2 sharps), 4/4 meter signature

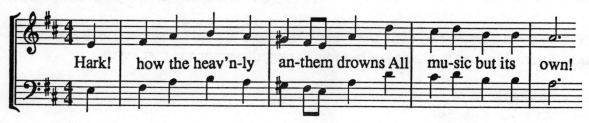

God of Our Fathers

Key of Eb major (3 flats), 4/4 meter signature

Of shin -ing worlds in splen -dor thru the skies...

Other Keys

Frankly, this has been a lot to absorb. If you really want to know this material, you will need to memorize the facts about keys found in this chapter. On the other hand, let us remind you that you don't really have to "know" all this information: You just need to understand it.

With that in mind, we are going to take a peek at some other keys you will encounter. Don't dwell on them. Just recognize that they will rear their heads from time to time.

A major (3 sharps) E major (4 sharps) Db major (5 flats)

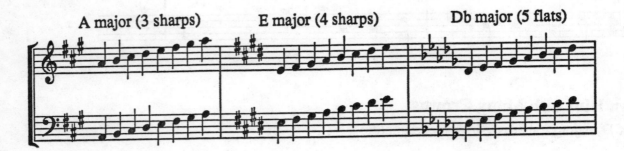

Of these three, the first two will rarely show their faces in your literature. Db, however, is not too uncommon. For instance, here are just few hymn titles written in that key:

Beneath the Cross of Jesus
I'd Rather Have Jesus
Jesus Paid It All
Just As I Am
Lead On, O King Eternal
Savior, Like a Shepherd Lead Us

however. You can sing the same tune in many different keys. That's called "transposition," just in case you wanted to know. We gave you an example of that earlier with "Amazing Grace" — once in G major and again in F major (a whole step lower).

As you move from hymnal to hymnal, anthem to anthem, you will likely encounter this reality — the same piece, but in different keys. Don't be surprised.

In addition, you will notice in many of your anthems that the keys will change at least once before the piece is finished. The composer/arranger will "modulate" from one key to another. Most likely, the key change will move up a half step (such as from C up to Db or G up to Ab.) Check it out the next time that happens and see if we're right.

Things to Remember

Sharp
Flat
Key signature
Accidentals
Natural

Chapter 5

Name More About That Tune

You've noticed that in several of our examples so far, the melody has strayed off the staff a little. We've pointed out a few notes here and there, hoping that you would forgive those little surprises and wait for this chapter to get some guidance. Thanks for your patience.

Regardless of your voice part, you're going to be singing a few notes above and below the staff. It happens to everybody, just like taxes. Some of those notes are on leger lines just like our lovable middle C. Let's look at them and learn them.

First, here are the notes adjacent to the staff:

Since the bass staff is for the basses (and sometimes the tenors), only the guys need to memorize the names of their adjacent notes. You tenors are never going to be asked to sing the lowest note, so you can skip it altogether; but that upper one will show up constantly. Let's give these notes male names. How about Fred ("F") and Bill ("B"). If it works ...

Now for the ladies. Sopranos will have to learn both of your adjacent notes, but the altos will never have to sing the top one. To stay with our gimmick, let's call your notes Donna ("D") and Gaile ("G").

More Leger Lines

There's more. Besides those notes adjacent to the staff, you will have to sing some that lie on more imaginary ladder rungs — leger lines. Learn what you'll need from the illustration that follows.

There are many more leger lines above and below each staff, but these are the ones you are most likely to encounter. For the fellows, remember that they run from "E" to "E" (catchy); for the ladies, remember that they run from "A" to "C" (not so catchy, but easy enough).

Basses, you will seldom be asked to sing that high "E," but it will happen periodically. It seems that in contemporary Christian music, all the guys are expected to sing in that range with freedom. In traditional Christian music, however, the basses get to remain lazy. Bet you'd like to argue that one.

Sopranos, that top "C" is for the very high singers. It ain't for everybody. Unfortunately, there are plenty of sopranos around who think they can sing that note. If you have the range and the control to do it, hallelujah. Otherwise, pick what we call the "second soprano" part (sopranos who sing harmony notes about three degrees lower than the first sopranos) and spare us the shattered glass.

Here is a little leger line practice for you. The note names are above the staff; the scale degree numbers are below.

Let Us Break Bread Together on Our Knees
Key of Eb major (3 flats)

The First Noel
Key of D major (2 sharps)

Joy to the World
Key of Ab major (4 flats)

Amazing Grace
Key of Bb major (2 flats)

New Starting Notes

Starting on 5

Another little detail that we slipped in on you without much fanfare concerns the starting note of the melody. When we first started naming that tune, the first note was always the key note. In "Joy to the World," for instance, we gave you the illustration in C major. The first pitch on the word "Joy" was a "C" (8th degree), making it easier for you to find and hear the descending C major scale.

Things are not always that simple. As you've noticed by now, the first note is often something other than the key note. If you are not singing the melody at all — singing alto, tenor, or bass instead — then it is highly unlikely your first pitch will be the key note. (Unless you're a bass. You guys do get some breaks occasionally.) We'll explore those problems later.

Here are some samples of former illustrations where you started on a different degree of the scale.

All Hail the Power of Jesus' Name

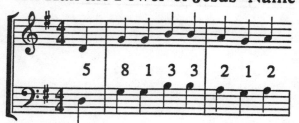

Amazing Grace

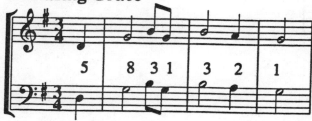

What do these two have in common (besides being in the same key)? They both start on the 5th degree of the scale and jump up to the 8th degree (key note). Remember that we pointed out this skip as one you would encounter often. Sharpen your hawk eyes and zero in on that pattern. Memorize its sound.

Here are some new examples of the same idea.

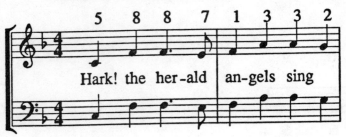

A lot of melodies begin on 5, but not always on the 5th degree below the key note. Many, in fact, begin on the 5th degree above. We've already encountered some of them. For instance...

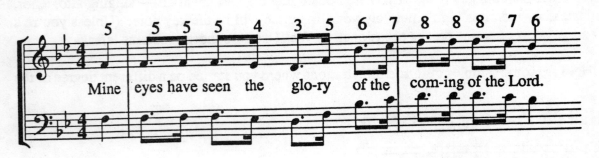

Here are some others you'll recognize.

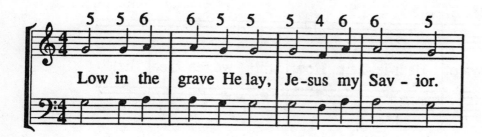

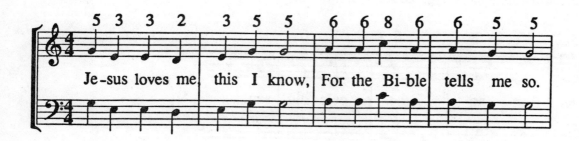

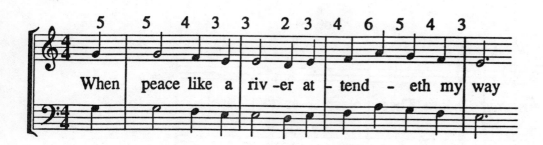

Starting on 3

Just as a lot of melodies begin on 5, many more begin on 3. Here are two examples we used earlier that started on the 3rd degree of the scale.

Have Thine own way, Lord! Have Thine own way.

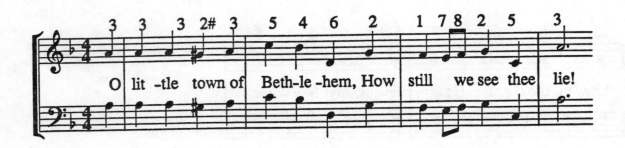

O lit -tle town of Beth-le -hem, How still we see thee lie!

Here are some new ones with the same condition.

The first no -el the an-gels did say...

(notice)

Near - er, my God, to Thee, Near - er to Thee!

Seek ye first the king - dom of God

Other than the key note (1st or 8th degree of the scale), these two starting pitches — 5 and 3 — are the most common you will find. They belong to their own little club. You don't really have to know what their qualifications are for membership in that club, but we'll tell you, anyway. Those three pitches (1, 3, & 5), when sounded simultaneously, form the most common chord in music — the triad. Without that basic chord of three notes, we would have chaos.

Back to our melodic discussion. You will find 1-3-5 frequently appearing in ascending order, but they are also found descending (5-3-1). You should memorize the sight and sound of these patterns -- 1-3-5 and 5-3-1. Here are some crutches you may lean on to help you,

Sing these over and over. Notice that "The Star Spangled Banner" gives you the descending and the ascending cluster in succession. That's a handy little crutch. Sing them with numbers and listen to yourself carefully as you do. You are establishing friends for life.

Now let's look at some variations on this theme. While these three prevalent notes often come in the neat package of 1-3-5 ascending and 5-3-1 descending, they have a way of jumping around a bit. They may frequently appear as 1-5-3, 3-1-5, or 3-5-1. Anything to keep you guessing.

Here are some good examples of these mixtures. Sing them with numbers and hear how these three colleagues interact.

(notice 6/8 meter signature)

(notice quarter rest at beginning)

Octaves

The distance from the 1st degree of the scale to the 8th degree is called an **octave**. Just as an octopus has eight arms, an octet has eight singers, and an octagon has eight sides, an octave has a total of eight lines and spaces from the starting note to the ending note.

Frequently we move in our melodies from 1-8 or 8-1 in stepwise motion (as we have seen and heard in "Joy to the World"). But you may get there in a number of other ways. The most common scenario is by means of the 1-3-5 or 5-3-1 pattern.

The example of "The Star Spangled Banner" is great for demonstrating this. Take another look.

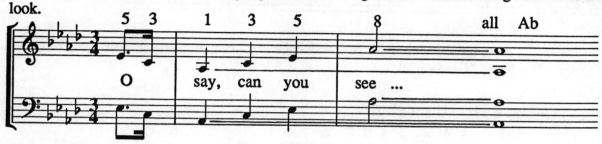

Here's another familiar example.

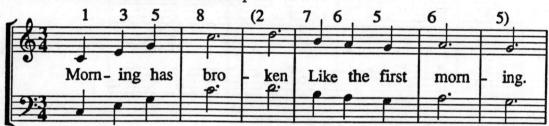

Again, memorize the sound of the octave. Learn to spot the 1st and 8th degrees easily, relying on them as your musical anchors. You can bet that 3 and 5 will show up shortly thereafter to join the party.

Sequence

Repeated notes and repeated patterns in your melodies will always make music reading more fun. The musical term for this is **sequence** — repeated melodic patterns, but at different pitches.

We pointed out the sequential pattern of notes in "God Is So Good" before. Here it is again.

One of the most famous examples of a sequence in Christian music is from the Christmas carol "Angels We Have Heard on High."

Angels We Have Heard on High

You will find sequences appearing regularly. Whenever you do, mark them on the music with your pencil. You could circle them and label "sequence," or you could use a bracket above the notes as we did in our example. Whatever your method, know that these patterns will speed you along the way to musical competence. So pray for a sequence or two.

Things to Remember

Fred and Bill
Donna and Gaile
1-3-5, 5-3-1
Octave
Sequence

Chapter 6

It's More About Time

Music has a pulse — a heartbeat. When we described it to you before, we said that it could be fast, slow, or somewhere in the middle — just like your own body's pulse. The important factor is that is must be <u>steady</u>. Does that sound familiar?

Well, the musical term we didn't mention at that time is **tempo**. That refers to the speed at which a piece of music should be performed.

For choirs, the tempo is usually selected and maintained by the conductor. So why are we bothering you with it? Because in learning to read music, you have to learn to read elements on the page which tell you how the music is to be implemented. Among those elements are tempo markings.

Now get this: The tempo might change in mid stream. You might be expected to get faster or slower. Not only do you need to understand how fast is fast, you also have to understand when fast becomes slow. Life is like that sometimes.

It's not done with mirrors: It's done with words. Where are they found? Right at the beginning of the piece of music in the upper left corner. They are also posted along the way just like speed limit signs.

In contemporary music literature published for the English-speaking world, you will usually find English words that have no ambiguity. For instance, you might see "slow" or "slowing." You might be invited to move "quickly" or "faster." Or you might be given a mood suggestion that will help guide the speed such as "prayerfully" or "with excitement."

That's about as challenging as pushing an elevator button, so we professional musicians had to find some way to give you grief. Our solution was to continue using the *original* words by the *original* composers in their *original* language. Welcome to the world of Italian!

If your Italian vocabulary consists of pepperoni, mushrooms, and extra cheese, you need some help. This is going to require some memory work on your part. Here is a handy list of the most common words you'll see.

Slow Speed:	*Lento, Largo*
Medium Speed:	*Andante, Moderato*
Fast Speed:	*Allegro, Animato, Vivace*

What hymn titles come to your mind when you hear *Lento (slowly)*? How about "Fairest Lord Jesus?" *Andante (medium speed)*? Try "The Doxology." *Allegro (fast)* ? Go for "Standing on the Promises."

There are some standard anthems in our choral literature that most choirs know. Let's see if we hit any titles in your repertoire. *Largo*? "God So Loved the World" by John Stainer. *Moderato*? "How Lovely Is thy Dwelling Place" from Brahms' REQUIEM. *Animato*? "With a Voice of Singing" by Martin Shaw.

Have you noticed how subjective these terms are? There are vast degrees of interpretation in how fast "Hallelujah" from MESSIAH should go. So a neat little device was invented to help musicians know exactly how fast the composer desired to hear his composition. It's called a metronome. If you've ever had piano lessons, you'll remember that little ticking box that drove you crazy before your time. It unforgivingly kept an exact and audible beat for you at whatever speed you set it to indicate.

At the beginning of the music, you may see a note value (often a quarter note), an equal sign, and a number. That is the metronome speed. When you see quarter = 60, the piece is supposed to move at one beat per second. When you see 120, it's exactly twice as fast. We've already given you a suggestion on how to find 60. Here's one for 120. John Phillip Sousa's "Stars and Stripes Forever" is supposed to move at 120 to a quarter note. Whistle it and tap your foot at the same time. That should put you pretty close to 120 — two beats per second.

Changing Speeds

Music would be boring if it always moved at the same speed like that monotonous metronome. Just as our moods change, causing our heart rates to vary, so the music has increases and decreases in speed.

Here comes another Italian lesson. The most common words for these indications are ...

Gradually slow down:	*Ritard, Rallentando*
Gradually speed up:	*Accelerando*

These are usually abbreviated in the score, so you need to learn how they will appear.

Ritard = *Rit.*
Rallentando = *Rall.*
Accelerando = *Accel.*

After you've been asked to change your pulse rate one way or the other, you may be asked to get it back where it was. The indication for returning to the original speed is *A Tempo*. The letter "A" there is pronounced "Ah," as in the word "far."

Tie

As we continue some more considerations about time in music, we need to discuss a very important device in rhythmic notation that you will encounter many, many times. It's called a **tie**. This is nothing more than a curved line that connects two note heads together. It looks like this:

Whenever you see a tie, it will always be connecting notes on the <u>same</u> pitch — the same line or space on the music staff. The function of the tie is to add the value of the two notes together. Two quarter notes tied together, each worth one beat, would result in one sound lasting two beats. So why don't they just write a half note, you ask? Good question. Usually the tie is used to connect two notes over a bar line. So the last note of one measure is connected to the first note of another. Here is a little sample.

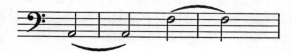

When we gave you the example of "Have Thine Own Way, Lord" earlier, we cheated. There was supposed to be a tie in that melody, but we left it out on purpose. You can peek at it on page 54, if you want. Here it is again, notated correctly.

Let's look at a few more examples of ties. Count the rhythm of each piece as you speak it and then as you sing it. Remember to set a good tempo and keep it steady.

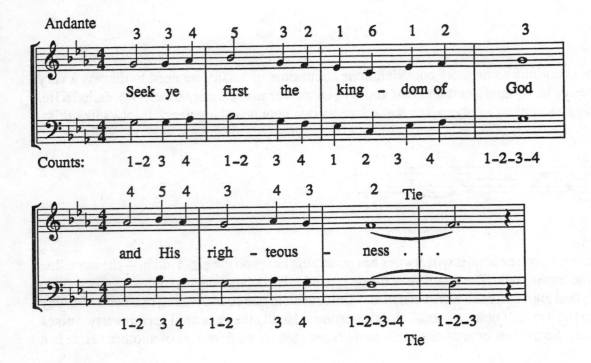

Caution: Don't confuse the tie with a very similar item called a **slur**. The slur looks almost exactly like a tie, but it is used differently. It connects notes of <u>different</u> pitches — not the same pitch. It's function is to alert you that a group of notes are to be performed together in a phrase — usually on the same syllable of a word.

Here are two examples of slurs. The first is one of the most common of all -- the two-note slur. The other example is of an extended passage you will recognize immediately.

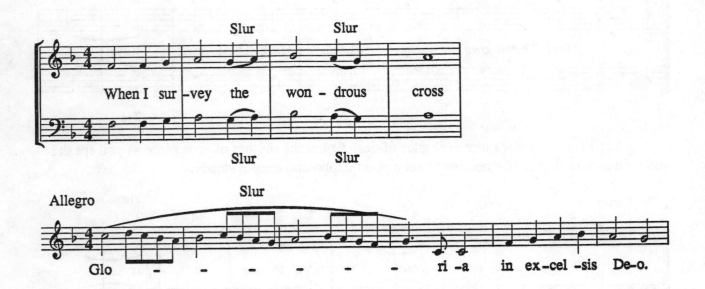

Things to Remember

Tempo
Lento
Largo
Andante
Moderato
Allegro
Animato
Vivace
Rit.
Rall.
Accel.
A Tempo
Tie
Slur

Chapter 7

Name Even More About That Tune

The Minor Scale

There is great beauty in music, but perhaps nothing as lovely as the **minor scale.** We've told you all about the major scale with its arrangements of whole steps and half steps. That's the one you will use 80% of the time (if not more). But there is also the enticing minor scale to discover. It will indeed show up, and you need to be ready for it.

Before you panic, we are not going to give you a heavy trip with this scale. You are not going to have to learn scads of key signatures and sing through droves of examples. This lighter touch will give you just what you need to move on. See? Now you can relax and enjoy.

The minor scale, like the major, is a progression of consecutive notes, either ascending or descending. It, too, consists of whole steps and half steps. Whereas the half steps in the major scale fall between 3-4 and 7-8, the minor scale has a different plan. The half steps fall between 2-3 and 5-6. Here is the one that has no sharps or flats — A minor.

In order to hear this sound, let's turn to some very familiar melodies using it. To keep it thematic, we'll use all Christmas carols.

Can you hear that different sound? It has a quality far removed from "Joy to the World" or "The First Noel." Some people describe the minor scale as sounding sad. That can be very true. Sing through the examples again and think "sad." Does that help in hearing the quality of the scale? Then, if you must, think sad.

Bad news: You can't tell a minor key from a major key by just looking at the key signature. In fact, they share key signatures. Those keys that do so are called **relative minors**. You don't have to remember that, but do grab the essence of it.

The key of A minor, which we gave you above, has no sharps or flats. What major key shares that characteristic? Right — C major. So they are relatives.

The three carols above were all originally written with one sharp in the key signature. Do you remember which major key has one sharp? You can look back, if you have to. This is not a quiz — just a reminder. The answer is G major. The name of the relative minor for G major is E minor. So the first degree of the scale for these carols should be "E." Let's transpose them to their real key and take a look.

Here's one other thing to remember about minor scales. There is often a tendency to add an accidental to this scale: The 7th degree is often raised a half step. How do you raise a note by a half step? Add a sharp. So in A minor, which has no sharps or flats in its key signature, it is not uncommon to see a G sharp — the 7th degree of that scale.

In "What Child Is This," you see an example of that raised 7th degree early in the melody. Remember, that melody is in E minor. The 7th degree is the one found a half step below "E." That means the "D" would be sharped, if the composer decided he liked that sound. Take a look at it and sing it through. Take a lingering moment on that D sharp (right around the words "on Mary's lap") to get the sound of it in your ear. You might find it helpful to raise one shoulder a bit when you sing it. No kidding! There's a definite "feel" to that raised 7th degree.

Intervals

Now, my friend, we come to the main course. Not that your appetizers, soups, and salads have been unimportant. It's just that you've needed all that has come before so you can happily enter the world of **intervals**.

Reading music would be too easy if all you had to do was sing scales up and down. All that stepwise motion would tranquilize you into La La Land. You have to sing skips, too. We've advised you to catch sight and sound of the skip from 5 to 8. Now we're going to examine many of the other possibilities.

An interval is the distance between two notes. When we sing from the 1st scale degree to the 2nd, the interval is called a second. Convenient. If you sing from the 5th degree to the 8th degree, what do you call it? The answer lies on the staff itself. You simply count the lines and spaces.

Start with the line or space on which you find the bottom note, count upward, and the resulting number gives you the answer. For instance, in C major, the 5th degree is on "G," and the 8th degree is on "C." Count the lines and spaces from "G" to "C" and find out how far it is.

The answer is four lines and spaces. So the distance is that of a 4th. (See next page.)

Don't confuse the scale degree numbers here with the number of lines and spaces between notes. We are still talking about scale degree 5 up to scale degree 8, but we start counting the 5th degree as 1 because we are measuring distance at this point. If you don't understand that, go back a few paragraphs and walk through this point one more time.

When you can spot intervals in your music and respond to them with your voice, you're going to experience your ability to read music taking giant steps forward. That's why we call this your main course. In order to do that, you have to have lots of practice. But we have some goodies for you that are going to make interval hunting more fun. Just as we have given you some crutches to lean on when learning 1-3-5 and 5-3-1 (remember "The Star Spangled Banner"?), we have some crutches for the primary intervals you will need to know. **Learn these. Know them cold.** You will use them constantly, and they will set you free in music land.

Before we share these crutches, we need to say something else. Really learning all about intervals means that you would have to master a significant amount of music theory. Your brain would need a built-in pitch pipe or, better yet, a computer. That's not the scope of this course, so we want to set you at ease a bit.

When your eye sees the interval of a third, for instance, you are not going to know whether it's a major third, a minor third, or one of several other possibilities. For those of you who want to get into this at that level, we'll give you some pointers at the end of this chapter. For the rest of you, take heart. If you can sing the scale, you can find most of the intervals you'll encounter in the music using the helps below. Most of the notes you will sing will fall somewhere on that musical scale.

Now here are the primary ascending intervals you will meet most often and our crutches to help remember their sounds. Some of them are already familiar to you. Sing these over and over. Memorize the crutches, the names, the sounds.

Ascending Intervals

Minor 2nd	Sing the 7th & 8th scale degrees of the scale
Major 2nd	Just sing the scale upward ("Do Re Mi") or the beginning of "When I Survey the Wondrous Cross"
Major 3rd	"Holy, Holy, Holy" - first two words = Major 3rd
	"What Child Is This" - first two words = Minor 3rd
4th	"Here Comes the Bride" or "Amazing Grace" (first two notes)
5th	"Holy, Holy, Holy" - first and third words.

Major 6th	"My Bonnie Lies Over the Ocean" (first two notes) or
	"It Came Upon a Midnight Clear"
Octave	"Bali Hi" from SOUTH PACIFIC (first two notes)

Let's put these into musical notation. For ease of learning, we'll write all of them in C major for now.

Notice that we didn't call the 4th or 5th "major" or "minor." That's because they go by another name — "perfect." You don't really need to remember "perfect 4th" or "perfect 5th" to sing them, however. Also notice that the only minor intervals included are the minor 2nd and minor 3rd. There are minor 6ths, and 7ths, but you will not encounter them as often.

Not all intervals move upward; they also descend. Here are the primary descending intervals you will encounter and some crutches for learning them.

Descending Intervals

Minor 2nd	Just sing the scale degrees 8 to 7
Major 2nd	Just sing the scale from 2 down to 1
	(If it helps, start with 1 up to 2, then turn around
Minor 3rd	"Star Spangled Banner," first two notes
Major 3rd	"Star Spangled Banner," second and third notes
Perfect 4th	"Here Comes the Bride" — in reverse ("Comes Here")
	or "O Come, All Ye Faithful" (first two notes)
Perfect 5th	"Star Spangled Banner" (first and third notes)
Major 6th	"Nobody Knows the Trouble I've Seen"
Octave	"It Came Upon a Midnight Clear"
	on the third line, "Peace on the earth"

Here are these intervals in musical notation, again using the key of C major.

Now let's look at some musical examples in their original keys and note their intervals. Use these examples as learning opportunities. The more carefully you study and sing them, the more you will gain for later application. A word about the abbreviations. "Major" is abbreviated by a capital "M;" "minor" is abbreviated by a lower case "m;" "perfect" is abbreviated by a capital "P."

So M3 = Major 3rd   m3 = minor 3rd   P5 = Perfect 5th

O God, Our Help in Ages Past

O Come, All Ye Faithful

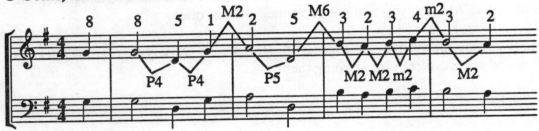

Great Is Thy Faithfulness

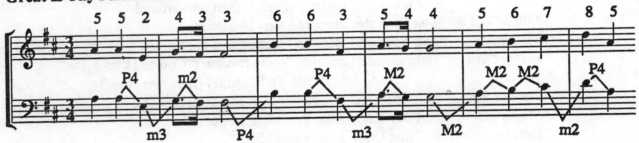

Love Divine, All Loves Excelling

Interval Qualities

For those of you who want to dig a little deeper, we are including here the basic information you need for determining the quality of an interval. That means developing the ability to determine if the interval is major, minor, or something else. As we mentioned before, this information is not necessary for the training of your musical ear for our purposes, but it's here for those who like to cross "t's" and dot "i's." Skip it, if you want.

You will often encounter minor intervals, even within a major key. Let's take the key of C major once again. Everything measured from the first degree of "C" will be either a major interval or a perfect interval. But what happens when you begin measuring from the second degree of "D?" Things can change.

You have to lay aside the fact that you are in the key of C major and start thinking in D major. After all, you are now measuring from the note "D." That means you have to know the number of sharps or flats normally found in the key of D major. We shared that information in Chapter 4. Whether you want to memorize all of it for this application is up to you. A really complete music reading skill would require it.

D major has two sharps. They are "F#" and "C#." In the key of C major — no sharps or flats — let's look at the intervals above the note "D." Remember, count "D" as 1 so that you can measure upward from there.

The first interval that's different is the 3rd. Since D major has an "F#" in it, while C major has a natural "F," we have an alteration. This is still a 3rd, but it is one half step smaller than the major 3rd we would have from "D" to "F#." It is therefore a minor 3rd.

The same of true of the 7th. D major has a "C#," but it is a natural "C" in the key of C major. The interval is therefore a minor 7th.

Just so you'll have the data for reference, we've taken all the other pitches of the C major scale and listed the intervals that lie up to one octave above them.

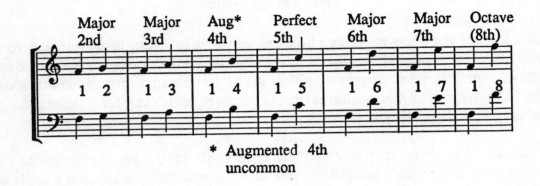

* Augmented 4th
uncommon

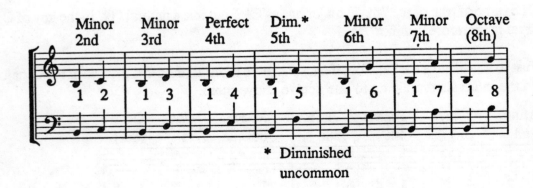

* Diminished
uncommon

If this were going to be an exhaustive diagram, we would have to investigate "C#," "Eb," "Ab," and all the other possible pitches. We would also need to discuss what are called "augmented" and "diminished" intervals. You can see how involved one could get with this whole process. That's what music degrees are for. If you can be satisfied with the rudiments, then just learn the crutches we shared earlier and move on. You will still be able to increase your music reading skill and enjoyment a hundred fold.

To close out this introduction to intervals, we've included some practice drills for you. Examine each interval and fill in the blanks. The answers are given at the end of this chapter. Don't worry: They are basic, common intervals. There are no trick questions.

Notice that we've included each note in four different octaves. That's to help acquaint you with some more lines and spaces. Also note that there are key signatures to think about for most of these examples. Trace from the key signature all the way across the staff to the right to check and see if the note should be a sharp or a flat. Have fun.

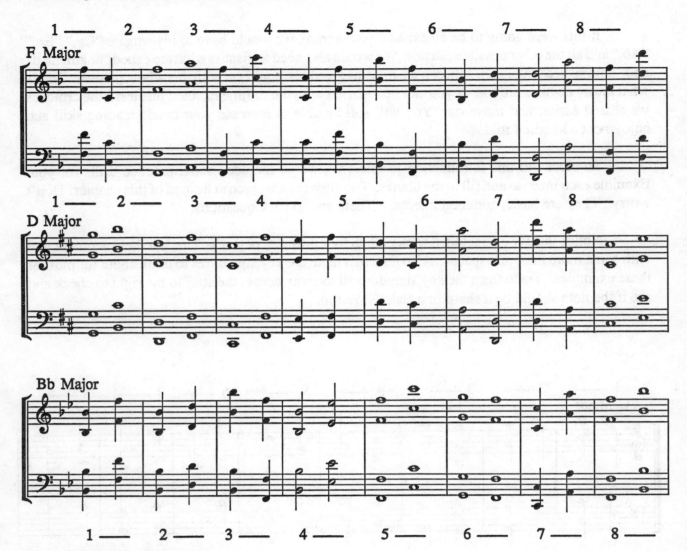

Things to Remember

Minor scale
Intervals
All crutches for intervals

Answers to interval drill:

	1	2	3	4	5	6	7	8
C Major	P5	M3	M2	M3	P4	P4	m3	P4
G Major	M3	P5	M6	P5	m2	M3	P4	m2
F Major	P4	M3	P5	P4	P4	M3	P5	M6
D Major	M3	M3	P4	M2	m2	P5	P4	m3
Bb Major	P5	M3	P4	P4	P5	M2	M6	P4

Chapter 8

Name Those Tunes

As every good boy does know, singing in the choir means singing a harmony part. What is harmony? That is the third essential element of music, about which we are going to say very little.

Harmony exists when we successfully combine individual parts of something into a pleasing, orderly whole. That could be said of marriage, of a committee, or a recipe.

In music theory, harmony exists when we combine two or more notes at the same time. The best harmony is when those simultaneous notes are pleasing to our ears. That's no joke.

We mentioned near the beginning of this journey that every voice part — every person, if you will — in the choir sings melodies. The alto part is a melody. It may not be the main melody of the composition, but it is still a melody.

So learning to sing the harmony part may be simplified to the process of learning to sing several different melodies at the same time. That's by individual singers, of course. Not that you needed to have that pointed out, but one never knows.

In four-part harmony, there are four tunes vying for attention simultaneously. Your job is to find your tune and stay on it. There are two challenges in that statement. First, you need to know where your part is located on the printed page. Then you have to sing it while all those other folks are doing their thing. Let's start with the first challenge. It's by far the easiest.

In a standard hymn, there are two lines of music. These are designed to be both played and sung. The top line of music is for the pianist's right hand while the bottom is for —you guessed it — the left hand. Those two lines also have the four melodies for the sopranos, altos, tenors, and basses. It would be surprising if you didn't already know that much, but we thought it best to double check. On the next page, you'll see how this scheme appears in print.

The ladies' voices (SA, standing for soprano and alto) share the top staff; the gentlemen (TB, standing for tenor and bass) are portioned to the bottom staff. Let's break this apart into four separate melodies. Find your voice part below and sing through your melody using numbers.

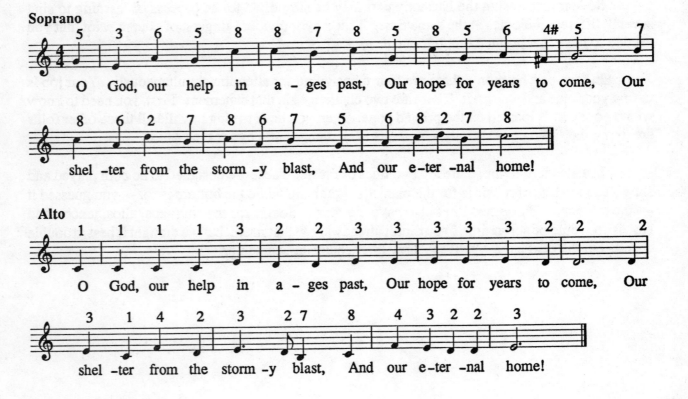

Only the soprano part here has the lead melody (the "tune"), so only the soprano part sounds like what we think of as "O God, Our Help in Ages Past." But the altos, tenors, and basses have the other three melodies that compose the harmony of this outstanding hymn. It's a little like scrambled eggs. The four eggs cooked together make a delicious concoction.

If you take a closer look at these parts, you will discover something typical. The alto melody doesn't move very far. The soprano, tenor, and bass melodies have many more skips with which to contend than the alto part. We're pointing this out not to put down the altos, but to encourage more sopranos to give this part a try.

You see, there are many sopranos who can and should sing alto. They freeze, however, at the prospect of having to read the alto notes. Yes, ladies, you will have to read them. But you are already having to read your soprano notes. What you really fear is your ability to remain independent on that alto part. Right?

Your experience tells you that your ear will hear the main melody (soprano notes), and you will stray back across the aisle into that familiar territory.

That's understandable. It's also lazy. It takes a little more patience and a little more effort to sing a harmony part when you are accustomed to singing the lead melody. Let's avoid saying that it takes a little more intelligence. That's not really true, but it is tempting to think that way. The fact is that alto part itself is usually not all that difficult. Becoming independent as an alto, however, is a growth factor.

Let's get off this soap box and get back to basics. A hymn is one thing, but an anthem is another. You will receive music for choir that is laid out much like a hymn, but there will be others that are not. This is where the tenors have to be the most flexible. We'll explain.

First of all, the voice parts in anthems usually consist of two lines of music (just like a hymn) above two lines of accompaniment for keyboard. That makes for lots more confusion on the printed page at first glance. You simply have to train your eye to spot your part.

Here is a typical layout for a simple anthem.

"Ride On!" by C. Harry Causey, Beckenhorst Press

Notice the brackets on the left side of the page. The staves for the voice parts are grouped together by a square bracket; the accompaniment staves are grouped by a curly bracket. Obviously, the text is a tip off that certain parts are to be sung; but sometimes there are stretches of music with no text. If you're looking for a quick reference point to find the voice parts, look for those square brackets.

The tenors are still where they were for a hymn. They are still sharing a staff with the basses, written in the bass clef. Their flexibility factor comes with the next example.

You may also see some anthems with a different layout. Instead of having four lines of music — two for voices and two for accompaniment — there are six lines — four for voices and two for accompaniment. This has the disadvantage of making you search for your part over a much larger field of printed music. It has the advantage of isolating your voice part from the others, making your melody distinctively clear. It's also in this layout that the tenor part is usually moved to the treble clef.

A typical example of this arrangement looks like this:

"How Lovely Is Thy Dwelling Place" from REQUIEM by Johannes Brahms

Why are there two styles of printing vocal music? It has to do with the nature of the piece being printed. Sometimes the individual voice parts are so independent, they need to be printed separately. It's as simple as that.

Sometimes the men get to rest while the ladies do all the work. Now ladies, let's not have any catty thoughts at this moment. We're talking about those times in the music when only the sopranos and altos sing. The opposite is also true: There are times when the men sing alone without the women. You'll find the latter happening less often. Why? Because in the average church choir, the men are fewer in number and don't read music as well as the women. Sad, but true. Composers, arrangers, and publishers knowing this have often opted for giving the women more musical moments than the men.

When certain sections of the choir are to rest, the section that is expected to keep singing is marked in the score. You'll see little letters above the vocal lines such as "sop" (sopranos) or "ten" (tenors). You may just see the capital letter for one of the four voice parts — S or A or T or B. SATB is another way to spell "choir."

Regardless of when or where your part (melody) is found in the music, apply the number technique to reading it. Don't hesitate to write in some of the numbers here and there to help remind you of how it goes. Look for intervals. Write in some of them above or below the notes when it helps. Writing a 5th here or a M3 there can greatly increase your reading after the first time through. That's assuming you are achieving some aptitude at singing 5th's, 3rd's, etc.

As you swim through the delightful maze of part singing, you will need to perform the fascinating trick of listening to the other parts and tuning them out at the same time. You need to train your radar beams to your part almost exclusively. At the same time, you need to bounce your part off the others, measuring time and pitch in accordance with what the rest of the choir is having to do.

Reading Hints

What can you do to make part singing easier for yourself? Here are some practical suggestions. They cover more than just learning to sing your voice part. No matter how well you read music, a good choir member should follow these guidelines.

1. **Find your starting note.** This you do by first checking out the key note. If you can't decipher it from the key signature, look at the first few notes of the left hand in the accompaniment. They often outline the scale in which the piece was written. If the key does not change during the piece, then you can look at the very last note on the last page. Again, the bottom note of the left hand (and probably the bass part as well) will define the key note for you. If you find it helpful, write the name of that key note in the upper left corner of the music. Remember that it's #1 in the musical scale of this composition.

2. **Keep your eye on other parts and the accompaniment as much as possible.** Learn to find reference points in the music. For instance, your part is going to enter soon on the note "G." Find a "G" in another voice part or in the accompaniment that occurs just before you have to enter. Circle it. Now use it like a beacon to find your entrance pitch.

3. **Make healthy mistakes.** When you are not sure of yourself, you may tend to hold back. You wait for Bertha to sing your notes so you can follow along. There's no shame in being a follower, but you need to be a brave one. *Your director can't help you learn your part if he or she does not hear you stumbling with it.* So if you are going to sing it wrong in rehearsal, go ahead and sing it loud enough to be heard. By daring to stick your toe in the water, the end result will be hastened.

4. **Keep the pulse.** The music's beat will tick along with or without you. It's more fun if it's with you. Find the beat. Physically do something to help youself establish the music's pulse. You might lightly tap your foot, tap your finger on something, or gently nod your head or body in time to the music. Be careful to use this technique for rehearsals only: The choir would look pretty strange nodding, tapping, and rocking in the choir loft on Sunday. Learn to establish an inner clock — a secret metronome that helps you stay in time.

5.   Look ahead. Once your note is over, the next one is upon you. Try to establish the good habit of reading one, two, or three notes ahead. The more you do this, the easier it will become. You will flower as a better music reader, perhaps looking a measure ahead eventually. Advance scouting the notes will also cause you to turn the page sooner. The music does not pause for page turns — choirs do. You need to flip it over quickly.

6.   Recognize patterns in the music. Look for repeated notes, repeated phrases, and sequences. Find not only repeated pitches, but look for repetitions in rhythmic patterns as well.

7.   Use a pencil. Circle anything in the music that will help you do your job better. Circle reference notes (see #2), problem spots, dynamics, repeated notes, sequences, rhythmic patterns, and important comments by your director during rehearsal (such as, "Don't breathe in this measure.").

8.   Rehearse other voice parts — not just your own. It is likely that your voice part will have to sing the same phrases, the same texts, the same rhythms, the same dynamics as some other voice part. When the director is taking the altos through their paces, *silently* sing along with them. Your tenor part will have its turn before long.

9.   Rehearse at home. Have a private rehearsal in your favorite rocking chair. Sing through the music at your own pace. Read the words aloud just to become familiar and relaxed with them. Then speak them in the correct rhythm of the piece while you tap your foot to keep a steady beat. Check out all your circled spots in the music. Remind yourself of why you placed the mark there in the first place. Go over that section several times so that you won't be repeating mistakes at the next rehearsal.

10.   Have confidence. Sing with blessed assurance. You can accomplish more than you think. The more you think you can accomplish musically, the more success you will have.

Things to Remember

Square brackets
Curly brackets
10 Hints

Chapter 9

Map Reading

Reading music is not unlike going on a trip with a handy road map in hand. That printed blueprint is very helpful, if you can read it. But put it in the hands of someone who is not at home with maps, and you might be better off following your nose.

Unfortunately, too many church choir members can't read their musical maps. And they don't follow their noses -- they follow their ears. My hope is that they will begin to follow their eyes because of this book.

By now you should be well on your way to receiving your music map reading merit badge. Don't turn off your ears, of course: Just turn on your genius, using the tools you are learning.

There are a few more symbols and vocabulary words that should help you get to your destination. Without them, wrong turns are probable. So let's get out our musical compass and head in the right direction.

Dynamic Markings

Unless you are a teen-ager, music has more than one volume level. There are some abbreviated Italian words that express those desires with which you are probably familiar. Just in case, here are the ones you will meet most frequently.

f (forte)	**loud**
ff (fortissimo)	**very loud**
p (piano)	**soft**
pp (pianissimo)	**very soft**

There's an old joke about the novice choir member who thought "*p*" meant "powerful." Every time the frustrated director shouted "*p*," he just got louder. Don't let that be your blunder. Learn these four indications well and watch for them in your music.

There's another abbreviation that you often find with "*f*" and "*p*." It's "*m*" for "*mezzo*," which means "half." Let's substitute the word "moderately."

mf (mezzo forte)	*moderately loud*
mp (mezzo piano)	*moderately soft*

These are all subjective levels of volume, determined by the mood of the piece and the mood of the choir director. Sometimes they're determined by the mood of the accompanist who may be banging the piano too loudly. Smile and pray for them: It's not easy being the accompanist.

You will find these IDI's ("Italian decibel indicators") scattered all about the page of your anthems. Get out your trusty pencil and circle them. Then observe them, even if your neighbors don't. By the way -- IDI is not really a musical term, just an attempt to be cute.

Do you recognize the famous "echo" effect in the piece, "How Great Our Joy!"? It's done with dynamic markings.

Sometimes there's a desire to gradually increase or decrease the volume. This is accomplished by two more Italian words, usually abbreviated:

cresc. (*crescendo*)   **gradually get louder**
dim. (*diminuendo*)   **gradually get softer**

That second one is often called "diminish." That's an easier one to remember for the English speaking world and means exactly the same thing.

A shorthand method for indicating these two words has been devised. It's more popular than using the words themselves. The symbols look like this:

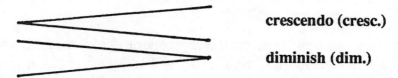

           crescendo (cresc.)

           diminish (dim.)

They work well visually, giving you a clear indication of what is needed. They have been referred to as "hairpins' — one opening, the other closing. That's not a technically recognized word in the halls of music conservatories, but you have our permission to use it anyway.

Accents

Music can be very dramatic at times. When that happens, you are likely to see **accent marks** with the notes. The most common accent mark looks like a little bird walked across the page.

When you see these markings, you are to punch the note. Do it with finesse, not with anger. Too many singers grunt out the notes when they see an accent mark. Very unbecoming.

Another less dramatic accent mark is the **tenuto mark**. It is just a short, straight line over the note that looks like this:

When you see these little dashes, they could mean one of two things. They could be a request to hold the note just a little longer than ordinary. The Italian word *tenuto* literally means "hold." That's certainly one way of accenting a note — holding it longer than the others around it. But the more likely meaning for this little accent is to "stress" the note slightly. In other words, just lean on it a little so that it stands out above the rest. Again, use discretion here. Make it subtle.

Triplets

There are some more symbols for your musical road map that have to do with time, not dynamics. We explored some of them in Chapter 6. Here are some new ones.

First, the **triplet**. You know that "triplet" refers to a grouping of three. On our map, it means three notes, of course. There is a bracket and the number "3" prominently signaling the arrival of the triplet, so you can't miss it.

There are two ways to define this rhythmic device — the hard way and the easy way. Let's do the hard one first. A musical triplet is defined as three notes to be performed in the time of two of the same value. What? Would you repeat that please? Well, suppose your triplet consists of three 8th notes. How many beats do two 8th notes usually receive? The answer is one beat — two 8ths equal one quarter note. So a triplet of three 8ths — receiving the same amount of time as two 8ths — equals one beat.

Confused? Well, here's the easy way to define it. Think of a triplet as three notes receiving one beat. The caution about this good-natured definition is that it's not always true. A triplet can sometimes equal two beats. The occurrences of that are not too common, however. You are most likely going to entertain the one-beat variety. So take your choice of definitions, but we would suggest the shorter one.

There are two famous instrumental examples of triplets you will probably recognize. The first is in the keyboard accompaniment to Bach's "Jesu, Joy of Man's Desiring." You can hardly attend a wedding without triplets. The second is in the trumpet fanfare introduction to each line of the hymn "God of Our Fathers." They look like this:

1-2-3   4 & d   1   2   3   4

Here are some other examples of triplets from choral music. We've included the counts to show you how to express them yourself — whether in writing or verbally. Try counting them out loud, tapping your foot for the basic pulse (beat) of each measure as you do. Note that the second example is one of those two-beat triplets that we mentioned.

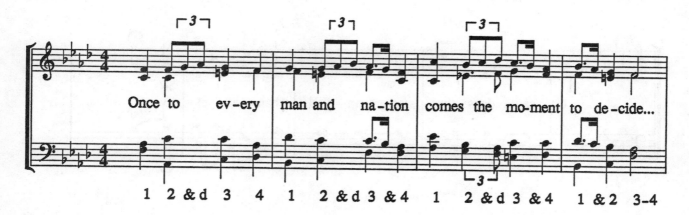

Fermata

Sometimes you need to hold a note longer than normal. To notate that desire, the composer uses a **fermata**. That symbol, facetiously referred to as a "bird's eye," looks like this:

How long you hold the note with the fermata is completely open-ended. There is a feeling for when it's right to move on. When in doubt, watch the director.

Here are some friendly fermatas you've undoubtedly seen before.

Take a look in your hymnal sometime at the hymn "He Leadeth Me." You will find a fermata at the end of every line.

Repeat Signs

It saves paper, time, and money to use **repeat signs** in the music whenever possible. Look for double bar lines with two dots that look like this.

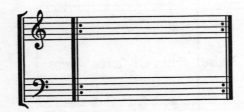

When you encounter a repeat sign, you bounce back to the beginning or to another repeat sign — whichever comes first. Then you sing the same material again. Here's an example:

Often, the repeat sign is part of a plan which involves a **first and second ending**. In this case, you will find the first ending marked with a bracket and a "1." The second ending is marked the same, but with a "2." You sing through the first ending to the repeat sign, go back to the beginning (or another repeat sign), and sing the material again. This time, however, you skip over the first ending and opt for the second. Here's an example:

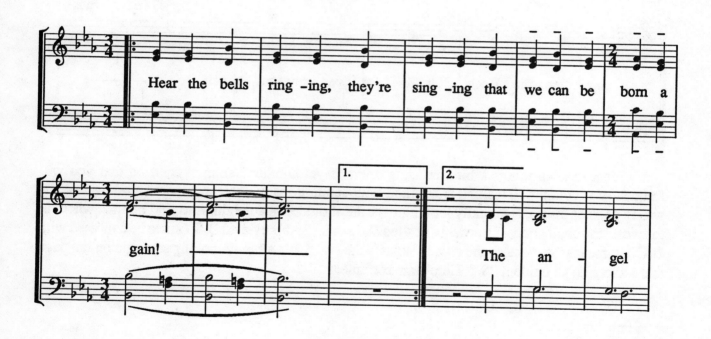

The Italians have again supplied us with some exotic ways to repeat musical material — *Da Capo* and *Del Segno*. Many choir members become confused by these markings, so pay special attention to them.

Da Capo, which is literally translated "the head," means to go back to the beginning of the piece (the head) and start over. Assuming that this indication is at the last measure of the last page, you could get caught in an eternal loop — always going back to the beginning and starting over, song without end. The solution is the Italian word *fine*. That's not the English noun for a fee or synonymn for the adjective "good": It is the Italian word for "finish." It's pronounced "fee-neh," with the emphasis on the first syllable. When you see it, you know you are finished, done, kaput.

Da Capo is usually abbreviated **D.C.** and has the word *fine* as a partner. They are connected by the Italian word *al* for "to." So finding *D.C. al fine* written over the last measure of your piece means "go back to the beginning (head), start over, and sing until you reach the word '*fine*.' Then stop." Aren't you glad we have such a brief way of saying all that?

There's a good example of this notation in the spiritual "There Is a Balm in Gilead."

Just to keep things a bit confusing, there is yet another Italian expression that you will frequently encounter. This one is credited with sending many choir members spiraling into the wrong page of music, frantically looking over the shoulder of a neighbor to find out just where in the world the choir is singing now. It's called *Del Segno*." Abbreviated **D.S.** (not to be confused with **D.C.**), it means "go back to the sign." What is the sign? It's a funny looking squiggle on the page that looks like an opulent "S." Here's an example:

What this means is that when you encounter **D.S.** in the score, you have to start looking backwards in the music for that sign. It will be well hidden somewhere between here and there, hiding among clusters of text, dynamic markings, and other unrepeatable Italian words, daring you to locate it. It will seem as if everyone else in the choir knows exactly where it is, and your intimidation factor will increase a hundred fold. Don't panic. Just calmly find the dumb thing. Then circle it. Put an asterisk by it. Draw an arrow to it. Dare it to evade you again. Note what page it appears on, then go back to that trifling **D.S.** message. Write yourself a note in the margin that says, "Back to page 2" — or whatever page you may need to revisit.

As if that weren't enough to cause you a neurosis or two, the **D.S.** and the **D.C.** messages also appear with the word **coda**. It will appear as *D.C. al Coda* or *D.S. al Coda*. A *coda* is a "tail." Just as *Da Capo* means to to the "head" of the composition, *al coda* means go to the "tail" or the ending.

When this happens, it's much like that elusive *Del Segno* sign. After you've gone back and started obediently repeating several pages of music, you will suddenly encounter the words *al coda*. That means you should immediately skip from wherever you are in the music, do not pass GO, do not collect $200, and resume what you were doing wherever you find that word *Coda* on the score.

Once you have found it, never let it go. (Sounds like Rogers and Hammerstein.) What page did you find *Coda* on? Go back to the spot that told you to go there in the first place and write another note — "Coda on page 7" — or whatever page is correct.

You know what? There's a certain amount of pride that creeps into the blood stream of anyone who can wrangle with all these repeat signs and symbols nonchalantly. Somebody should pin a *coda* on the donkey and put a crown on your *capo* to celebrate. Really, they are not difficult once you understand them. Then mark them. As you grow in the ability to read ahead, you'll see those markings and respond without missing a beat.

Application

It's time to bring all this into focus and see it applied to an anthem. John Stainer's "God So Loved the World" is a treasured anthem familiar to many. It's full of the notational devices we've been discussing. Hopefully, you've sung this before and can read through it with a fair amount of assurance. Our point is for you to look, see, and respond to the various notational devices you see there. Let's do it.

See next page

God So Loved the World - John Stainer

Things to Remember

f
ff
p
pp
mf
mp
Accent marks
Triplets
Fermata
Repeat signs
First ending
Second ending
Da Capo
Fine
Del Segno
Coda

Chapter 10

Name That Tune — for Real

Now that you've reached this point, you are ready for your driver's license in music reading. You're not ready to be a chauffeur, but you can get around the corner and over the bridge.

There is more — so much more — about music notation and music reading that one could learn. But we've attempted to give you what we think you'll need to do a fine job in your choir.

To give you some of that self confidence you need as a new driver, we're going to turn you loose with the keys and send you on a few short trips. We've included a number of sample melodies here for you to read. Some of these have appeared elsewhere in this driver's manual, but many of them are new.

Although we've given you a few tips here and there, we've printed the melodies just as you would find them presented to you in choir rehearsal or in a Sunday morning service. We've omitted the titles and the words, of course. They are all well known tunes which we hope you'll recognize as you start singing and counting. Just as in algebra, you will find the answers in the back of the book. Now don't cheat. Solve the problems first, then check yourself for accuracy.

Enjoy your new skill. Keep using it and watch it develop. And may the Lord, who has put the Song into this world, bless you in your ministry to Him through music.

> *"...The singers joined in unison, as with one voice, to*
> *give praise and thanks to the Lord."*
>
> II Chronicles 5:13

Example #1

Example #2

Example #3

Stately

Example #4

Example #5

Note 9/4 meter signature

Example #6

Example #7

Example #8

Example #9   (One note is deliberately wrong in this melody. Can you find it?)

Example #10

Example #11

Joyfully   (Two beats per measure, half note receives one beat.)

Example #12

(This melody does not start at beginning of song.)

Example #13

(Chorus)

Example #14   (Note 6/4 meter signature.)

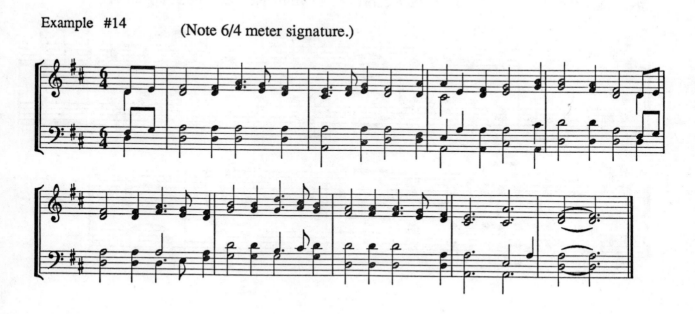

Example #15

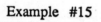

Example #16   (This is the chorus of a hymn. Note 9/8 meter signature.)

Example #17   (There's one note deliberately wrong in this melody. Can you find it?)

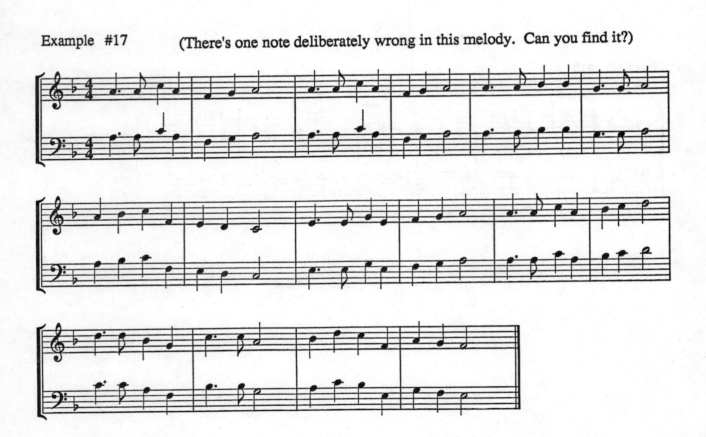

Example #18

Example #19

Example #20

Answers to musical examples

1. Jesus Loves Me
2. Go Tell It on the Mountain
3. A Mighty Fortress Is Our God
4. Joyful, Joyful, We Adore Thee
5. Have Thine Own Way, Lord
6. How Lovely Is Thy Dwelling Place
7. O Come, All Ye Faithful
8. Every Time I Feel the Spirit
9. He Is Lord
    (First line, last measure, the first note should be an "A.")
10. Jesu, Joy of Man's Desiring
11. The Joy of the Lord Is My Strength
12. There Is a Balm in Gilead
13. To God Be the Glory
14. Just As I Am
15. This Is the Day
16. Blessed Assurance
17. Come, Ye Thankful People, Come
    (Second line, first measure, the second note should be a "B natural.")
18. He Shall Feed His Flock
19. Hallelu
20. Blest Be the Tie that Binds

Glossary

Here is a handy reference list for the major items contained in this book. These definitions are designed for the singer who has studied the approach to music reading as found here.

A Tempo — Return to the original tempo or speed. (Chapter 6)

Accidentals — Sharps, flats, or natural signs that appear in music, usually beyond those found in the key signature. (Chapter 4)

Accelerando (accel.) — Indicates a gradual quickening of tempo. (Chapter 6)

Accent Marks — Various symbols near note heads indicating an extra emphasis on those notes. (Chapter 9)

Allegro — A speed indication meaning "lively and quick." (Chapter 6)

Andante — A speed indication meaning "moderate." Usually implies a steady beat and not too slow a speed. (Chapter 6)

Animato — A style indication meaning "animated." Connotes a quick tempo. (Chapter 6)

Bar Line — A short vertical line on the staff which divides the music into measures. (Chapter 3)

Bass Clef — The sign that indicates the staff used by the basses and often by the tenors. Defines the names of lines and spaces on the staff (lines: **GBDFA**; spaces: **ACEG**). (Chapter 1)

Beam — A line that connects two or more 8th or 16th notes. (Chapter 3)

Beat — The regular, steady pulse of a piece of music. The primary unit of rhythm. (Chapter 3)

Brackets — Vertical lines joining a family of staves found to the left of the printed score. Staves for choral parts are usually joined by square brackets; staves for accompaniments are usually joined by curly brackets. (Chapter 8)

Coda — ("Tail") A final ending to a piece. (Chapter 9)

Da Capo (D.C.) — "To the Head," meaning to return to the beginning of a piece. (Chapter 9)

Del Segno (D.S.) — "To the Sign," meaning to go back in the music until you find the sign indicating the starting point of a repeated passage. (Chapter 9)

Dot — Adds one-half of a note's value to itself. (Chapter 3)

Dynamic Marks — Words, abbreviations, and symbols in music indicating volume. (Chapter 9)

Eighth Note (8th Note) — A note with one hook on its stem equal to one-half the value of a quarter note. It is usually worth one-half of a beat. (Chapter 3)

Fermata — (Bird's Eye) A symbol extending the value of a note for an unmeasured length of time. (Chapter 9)

Fine — The indication for an ending in a composition which occurs somewhere other than the last measure. Usually found after the request to go back to the beginning and repeat part of the material. (Chapter 9)

Flat — A symbol (b) that lowers a note one-half step. (Chapter 4)

Forte (f) — Loud (Chapter 9)

Fortissimo (ff) — Very loud (Chapter 9)

Half Note — A note whose duration is equal to two quarter notes, therefore usually receiving two beats. (Chapter 3)

Half Step — The closest possible distance between two notes. Corresponds to the 7th and 8th degrees of the major scale. (Chapter 1)

Interval — The distance between two separate notes measured according to the number of lines and/or spaces between them. (Chapter 7)

Key Signature — An arrangement of sharps or flats at the beginning of a composition that defines on what scale the piece is built. (Chapter 4)

Largo — A speed indication meaning "slow." (Chapter 6)

Leger (Ledger) Line — A line written above or below the staff for notes beyond the range of the staff. (Chapters 1 and 5)

Lento — An speed indication meaning "slow." (Chapter 6)

Major Scale — An arrangement of eight consecutive pitches, both ascending and descending, containing whole steps and half steps. The half steps come between 3-4, 7-8. The first (1st) and last (8th) notes have the same name and define the name of the scale. (Chapter 1)

Measure — The distance between two bar lines, defined by the number of beats indicated in the top number of the meter signature. (Chapter 3)

Melody — A pleasing arrangement of consecutive notes. (Chapter 2)

Meter Signature — Two numbers, one above the other, found at the beginning of a musical composition. The top number defines the number of beats per measure; the bottom number identifies what type of note receives one beat. The most common meter signature is 4/4 — four beats per measure, quarter note receiving one beat. (Chapter 3)

Mezzo Forte (mf) — Moderately loud (Chapter 9)

Mezzo Piano (mp) — Moderately soft (Chapter 9)

Middle C — The note one leger line below the treble staff and one leger line above the bass staff. (Chapter 1)

Minor Scale — An arrangement of eight consecutive pitches, both ascending and descending, containing whole steps and half steps. The half steps come between 2-3, 6-7. The 7th degree is often raised one-half step by an accidental. (Chapter 7)

Moderato — A speed indication meaning "moderate speed." (Chapter 6)

Natural — A symbol that cancels the effect of a sharp or flat. (Chapter 4)

Octave — The eighth tone of a scale or the interval of eight notes with the bottom and top notes having the same name. (Chapter 5)

Piano (p) — Soft (Chapter 9)

Pianissimo (pp) — Very soft (Chapter 9)

Quarter Note — A note having one-fourth the duration of a whole note. The most common note in music. (Chapters 1 and 2)

Rests — Symbols in music that indicate measured silence. They correspond in value to the various notes (whole, half, quarter, 8th, 16th).   (Chapter 3)

Repeat Signs — Vertical bars with two dots encompassing a passage of music to be repeated. (Chapter 9)

Rhythm — A regular, orderly occurrence of beats causing a flow to music. (Chapter 3)

Rallentando (rall.) — Indicates a gradual slowing of tempo. (Same as Ritard) (Chapter 6)

Ritard (rit.) — Indicates a gradual slowing of tempo. (Same as Rallentando) (Chapter 6)

SATB — Soprano, Alto, Tenor Bass. Indications for the four voice parts of the choir. (Chapter 1)

Sequence — A succession of phrases based on the same melodic pattern but on different pitches. (Chapters 2 and 5)

Sharp — A symbol (#) that raises a note one-half step. (Chapter 4)

Sixteenth Note (16th note) — A note with two hooks (flags) on its stem, equal in value to one-half an 8th note. It is usually worth one-fourth of a beat. There are four 16th notes in one quarter note. (Chapter 3)

Slur — A curved line connecting two or more notes into a phrase. Usually found when two or more notes are to be sung on one word or syllable. (Chapter 6)

Staff — Arrangement of five horizontal lines and four spaces between them on which music is printed. (Chapter 1)

Skips — Notes that are separated by a distance greater than a 2nd. (Chapter 2)

Steps — Notes that lie adjacent to one another, either in half steps or whole steps. (Chapter 2)

Tempo — The speed of a musical selection. (Chapter 6)

Tie — A curved line connecting two notes of the same pitch, in effect linking them together and combining their separate values into one. (Chapter 6)

Treble Clef — The sign that indicates the staff used by the sopranos and altos. Also used for the tenor section occasionally. Defines the names of lines and spaces (lines: EGBDF; spaces: FACE). (Chapter 1)

Triplet — Three notes receiving the same value as two of like kind. Often three notes receiving one beat. (Chapter 9)

Vivace — A speed indication meaning "very fast." (Chapter 6)

Whole Note — A note whose duration is equal to four quarter notes, therefore usually receiving four beats. (Chapter 3)

Whole Step — The distance between two consecutive notes equaling two half steps. Corresponds to the first two notes of the major and minor scales. (Chapter 1)

About the Author

Having served as a church musician in a number of different churches for nearly 25 years, Harry Causey became a free-lance minister of music in 1981. That decision offered him the freedom to fulfill several dreams. One of those was to establish a national ministry to other church musicians, which he does through his company, **Music Revelation**. Another was the establishment of **The National Christian Choir** — a large, auditioned, interdenominational choir in our nation's capital.

Through Music Revelation, Rev. Causey publishes a monthly newsletter of the same name. The publication is dedicated to equipping and inspiration. He is in demand as a leader for choir retreats and worship workshops throughout America. His teaching materials include numerous audio cassettes as well as two other books — **Open the Doors to Creativity in Worship** and **Things They Didn't Tell Me About Being a Minister of Music.** Both books are best-sellers that have not only blessed thousands of church musicians but have found their way into the curriculum of numerous Christian colleges. The first book has also been released in album format as a book-on-tape.

Through The National Christian Choir, Rev. Causey is seeking to proclaim the glory of God through music to the entire nation and the world. The Choir has made four major recordings since their beginning in 1984. They have sung in the Kennedy Center, Constitution Hall, Washington's Convention Center, and The National Cathedral as well as in numerous auditoriums and churches in the Washington, D.C., area. They were the featured choir in Manger Square in Bethlehem on Christmas Eve, 1986. In the summer of 1990, they ministered in East Germany and Czechoslovakia. Plans call for them to make various tours to other parts of America as well. Recordings of The Choir are also available through Music Revelation.

Rev. Causey lives with his wife, Elizabeth, in Rockville, Maryland — a suburb of Washington, D.C. They have two children, David and Debbie.

If you are interested in inviting Rev. Causey to your church, or if you desire further information about his newsletter and other materials, you may contact him as follows:

Music Revelation
7 Elmwood Court
Rockville, Maryland 20850-2935
(301) 424-2956
FAX (301) 424-3955

Notes

Notes

Notes